UNDER THE OLD RAILWAY CLOCK

CAROLINE WHITEHEAD

By the same author:

Shadows In Every Corner

Surviving The Shadows

Rowland: A Heart of Sunshine

UNDER THE OLD RAILWAY CLOCK

Reminiscences of a time, a place, and
a very dear brother, William Marshall

CAROLINE WHITEHEAD

PUBLISHING HOUSE

151 Howe Street, Victoria BC Canada V8V 4K5

Note: To protect some individuals' privacy and to more effectively relate some stories, the author has used literary licence; some names and events have been changed or omitted.

For rights information and bulk orders, please contact
info@agiopublishing.com
or go to
www.agiopublishing.com

Under The Old Railway Clock
ISBN 978-1-927755-08-2 (paperback)
ISBN 978-1-927755-09-9 (ebook)

Cataloguing information available from
Library and Archives Canada.
Printed on acid-free paper.
Agio Publishing House is a socially responsible company, measuring success on a triple-bottom-line basis.
10 9 8 7 6 5 4 3 2 1 . 2

DEDICATION

To my dear friend Odette.
Your encouragement brings out the best.

ACKNOWLEDGEMENTS

To my family for their love and support
in whatever challenge I dare to face.

To my London, UK writers group, *Keep On Keeping On*.

To Bruce and Marsha Batchelor, Agio Publishing House, Victoria,
for their expertise in making this publication possible, and for the
design and cover of the book by award-winning artist Marsha.

Thank you, all!

PROLOGUE

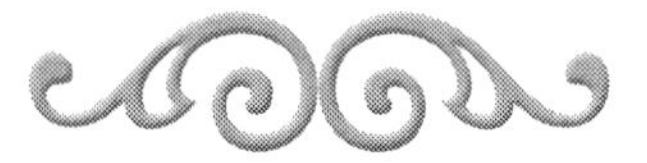

In 1933 at a summer holiday camp in Dymchurch, Kent, destiny deemed a ten-year-old boy and an eight-year-old girl would meet under the most bizarre circumstances.

The camp was the year's high point for children from the County's Catholic Church-run orphanages. After eating breakfast in the camp's large canteen, the impetuous young St. Anne's girl quietly slipped away from the other children, and from the camp's leaders, and went down to the beach, an area permitted only when requested, and out of bounds until such time. Watching and listening to the gentle waves of the incoming tide touching the shoreline, Caroline breathed in the salty ozone. Having had her fill of a relatively short taste of freedom, she clambered over the concrete sea wall and headed towards the playing fields. Casually strolling in the direction of the camp, she was alerted by a swish from above, as a football appeared from the sky and landed at her feet. She bent down to pick it up when a boy from St. Mary's about two years her senior approached and gruffly proclaimed, 'That's mine.'

The child was nonplussed. She picked up the ball and handed it to him. Without a word of thanks, he walked away toward the closest pitch. Deep in thought, the girl looked up and suddenly saw a camp leader rush toward her. Gripping Caroline by the arm, the leader called to the boy by name to come back. William stood at a distance and despite encouragement to move forward, he remained motionless.

What the camp leader was to divulge to the children, would change their lives forever. Pointing one finger at the girl, then at the boy, she said simply, 'You two are brother and sister.'

This bizarre isolated meeting in their childhood years would develop, in time to come, into a tight-knit relationship.

Where does one begin to put in words the character of a man, unique in his own style? Full of cheeky humour, my brother William Marshall often aggravated the spouses of the ladies who stopped to chat in Asda supermarket at Waterlooville with his suggestive remark, 'Meet me under the old railway clock, seven sharp.' I am sure he fancied himself back on ship as Petty Officer giving commands to seafaring ratings.

A proficient engineer and clock repairer, William's mathematical brain was reliable as a timepiece's pendulum when dealing with monetary problems. When calculating sums of money he was able to spot an error within a fraction of a penny. And he was always certain about the best odds for a bet – on a match or in life.

Apart from the difference in character of my two brothers – William gregarious, Rowland charismatic – they were one of a kind; both were caring and overly-generous when it came to family. William's marriage to Violet for 44 years was happy. To his children, he was a generous, loving father.

During the early years of his life, by a twist of fate, he briefly met a slender eight-year-old girl who unbeknown to him until that time, was one of his sisters. It was not until two of his three sisters attended a school reunion in the County of Kent, did that boy and girl chance to meet again, all of us now in our teen years.

A relationship, uncommonly strong between some siblings, developed throughout our lives with memories that often caused me to reflect that had this childhood incident not happened, brother and sister would have gone through life not even knowing the other existed and lived within reachable boundaries of each other. For we were all wards of the orphanages, left as infants without contact by our mother, knowing only as much of our origins – and any possible relatives – as the Sisters wished to reveal.

Throughout his 26 years service in His Majesty's Royal Navy, William develop a camaraderie with his fellow men with a carefree abandon, albeit, keeping his toes strictly on the line of protocol. In his quick action in dealing with a fire that started in the engine room, he not only saved the life of his captain, but also the ship and its entire crew. For his bravery, he was awarded a medal.

William was a man whose heart was larger than himself, someone who left his indelible mark on the world. No doubt those ladies at Asda, whom he suggested, 'Meet me under the old railway clock, seven sharp,' miss him too.

A LOVEABLE CHARACTER

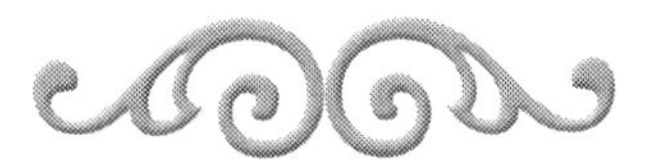

My brother William was born in Lambeth, North London, England, as the fourth child of Caroline Elizabeth Marshall. From the day we knew of each other and thereafter, our respect and love for one another grew stronger as the years progressed.

Of the genes he inherited from our mother, I wondered if the humorous part of his character stemmed from there. But, in essence, I rather fancy this trait came from the male side of the family. Among other hereditary qualities, Mother was apparently a gregarious lady of fashionable flair, difficult to contest. Quite impressed with her aunt's personality, my first cousin conveyed to me that Mother was a person of extreme generosity. Yet this was also a woman who callously cast away her own infant children to orphanages. Only the surface of Mother's character has been "scratched" from family research due to the fact she was unknown to her own children until she passed on in 1952.

The characteristics of who we siblings were, or who we are, continues to haunt the writer as the many versions of this woman's history still remain a mystery. I am consciously aware that the particles of dust of the deceased are silenced, forever.

A swaggering, charismatic man who loved to "bowl" over the ladies at every opportunistic moment, it never dawned on William to care that his style of approach to the opposite sex could please or displease them, as he charmed with endearments. Be it at the supermarket or in town, with a wink, his suggestive remark, 'See you tonight under the old railway clock at seven,' was a never-ending joke among the town people, particularly for his gambling cronies who knew him of old.

The antiquated clock to which he referred hung on the outside wall of the Portsmouth railway station and became a place where lovers met in silent tryst. At the appointed hour of seven, and at all other hours of day and night, it boomed the time and was heard for miles beyond the bustling naval town.

When the ladies curiously looked at him to wonder if his invitation was sincere, William returned their gaze as if to say, 'Well, are we on or not?'

Invariably, the lady or ladies in question "clicked" on to his amorous suggestions, knowing full well he was all talk and no action.

Often within hearing distance where William stood chatting, full of vim and vigour, to their wives, some of the grumpy old men stopped in their tracks to listen.

'What can you expect of him?' they moaned to one another.

'Typical Navy, blasting off like cannons in mid-ocean. It's nothing but hot air,' one called out, his voice reverberating throughout the store.

'A piece in every port,' snorted an old fellow, showing off his mouthful of large nicotine teeth and determined to get in his bit.

None took kindly to William and his innocent bantering; perhaps they were feeling threatened when he laughed and joked with their spouses or girlfriends as they stood in the aisles of the supermarket enjoying the latest neighbourhood gossip. Though fully aware of the disapproving glares and comments from their menfolk, William was not to be put off. He cajoled all the more, all the merrier.

His life philosophy: 'If you can't have a little fun in life, you might as well curl your toes up with a final *Amen*.'

The bantering went on throughout William's life, more so as he aged. Even with his limited energy due to on-going health problems he was determined to enjoy whatever years he had left. Over the decades, his invitations to ladies for marriage, gambling on the horses or meetings under the old railway clock at Portsmouth Station became progressively more bold, knowing he had little to lose. Any suggestion of stopping the wheels from turning would cause him to throw back his head and emit a loud belly laugh. As I listened to his lifestyle credo, I knew it was not on his agenda to stop and “give over”. The idea would be unimaginable. He would deem it as unlikely as someone taking the liberty of removing a cigarette from his mouth – his life and soul survival.

BACK TO THE BEGINNING

It was at the age of eight I met that ten-year-old boy with black hair, dark brown eyes and a grin on his face that stretched right across, in the playing fields at a holiday camp at Dymchurch, Kent.

My light brown curly hair, cut short to the tip of my ears, grew into soft rolls. Using sharp scissors, the person in charge of the girl's grooming cut off my hair in a style known as the "pudding basin". This procedure, to avoid long hair accommodating unseen "guests" on a child's head, was applied to all the girls at my school. As I listened to the scissors chop, chop and saw rolls of curls drop in a cluster to the floor, tears ran down my face. Pride, being a mortal sin, was considered the ultimate downfall of a girl who broke the laws of the Catholic church. I questioned my conscience, 'Did I really commit a mortal sin for wanting long curly hair?' After all, I was but a child.

Looking smartly dressed in grey shorts and a white shirt, his hair brushed off his forehead, the boy studied my face with his dark brown eyes. I was afraid to look at him, so remained dumb, thinking, 'What does he want with me? Who *is* he?'

I averted my eyes from his face. I wanted to run along the sandy beach and feel the soft white sand crunch between my bare toes. To sniff the ozone coming off the ocean, and breathe in deeply the salty sea air.

But the magic of the moment held me spellbound. Why was I wasting Nature's time on a sunny afternoon, standing mute in front of a young boy I didn't know? I wanted to watch the sun's rays glisten over the white foam above the waves, as they rose and fell in rhythmic motion to flow gently at the water's edge.

Suddenly, a motion caught the boy's eye. He recognized a woman of medium height, slim, in her mid-forties, as his camp leader, rushing towards him. Her arms were held high, waving frantically. I was about to run away, when the woman's voice demanded my attention.

'Stop!' was the command.

I held my feet to the ground, as though stuck in concrete.

Grabbing me by the arm, the woman led me to where the boy stood, looking expressionless.

Pointing from one to the other, she gasped out her words, 'You two are brother and sister.'

I struggled to free my arm from her hold, but the more I struggled the tighter she held on, as my face took on a bright red.

Thinking she had succeeded in getting the message across, the woman slowly let go of me. I fled the scene. Horrified and confused with what I had heard, I vowed never to see *that* boy again, and resolved to put the memory out of my mind.

The beautiful Dymchurch resort had sandy beaches stretching for miles along the shoreline. As the evening sun disappeared beneath the horizon, the lush green fields where hundreds of Romney Marsh sheep roamed freely, were silhouetted in beams of orange and red, casting a glow over the marshes that radiated for miles. Many children who came from different orphanages within the County went to the camp, and for two weeks enjoyed a comparatively unrestricted lifestyle. Most were of the opinion they were orphans. However, in years to come, this misinterpretation of a secret birthright was to rear its head in many forms.

After saying my morning prayers and eating a hearty breakfast in the large canteen, with a sense of pure joy, I slipped away from the "family" group to take a daily walk along the wide sandy shore. This freedom of movement on the beach or in the playing fields was permitted provided you let someone of authority know where you were going. And for how long a period. This sometimes caused children to overlap their time of freedom, when minds wandered within Nature's boundaries and the minutes didn't count. When this happened on a few occasions, my contrition to say a few more Hail Mary's did not disconcert me. On the contrary, young as I was, I felt exonerated.

The sheer ecstasy of being alone, to dwell absent-mindlessly without the distraction of man or beast, was Heavenly. The beauty of the landscape surrounding the holiday camp, I reasoned, was God's creation.

With the exhilaration of youthful energy, I jumped over the sea breakwall posts that jutted out from the top of the sandy beach to a hundred or more feet out to the ocean floor. When no one was in sight, my legs straddled these breakers from the tip of the sandy shoreline to the edge of the water. With every jump, my arms in the air, I laughed as though never wanting to stop!

Strong winds gusted off the Atlantic Ocean caused incoming tides to splash over the top of the concrete breakwater that extended for miles at the top of the beach, leaving salty puddles in its wake, forcing holidaymakers to walk along its narrow ledge and jump over them.

I looked skyward at the noise of the gulls, and watched as their wings dipped and dived over the crest of the waves, with precise aeronautical skill. The gulls, and other migratory birds, feed well on mackerel and herrings, abundant in these waters.

Between the months of April and September fishermen from the nearby villages of Lydd and Greatstone used a form of trapnet fishing, once common around the estuaries and sandy shores of the British Isles, and known as kettlenet fishing in the early 1890s to the late 1920s. Wooden poles, 16 feet long, were dug 3 feet into the sand, using special spades and forks. The idea being that two men, facing each other and digging together, could excavate wet, caving sand quickly, to dig a narrow deep hole to hold the pole which had its end bound with strips of rope or sacking, helping to hold the pole steady and upright once it was inserted into the prepared hole and sand trodden firmly around it.

Once the poles were held in place, the fishermen could hang the nets. When the tide came in, shoals of fish met this barrier of nets and instinctively they turned for deeper water and travelled along the range of net, straight into the kettle or bythe net, as it was called, becoming trapped.

Mackerel was the main catch of the kettlenets, but other species of fish were caught. A Thresher shark once caught in a net did not come as a surprise to the fishermen, knowing they were seen occasionally in these waters.

Hearing the sound of children's laughter coming from the fields, my innermost conscience warned me I had not obtained the permission of a staff member to leave the "family". I left the sandy beach, scrambled over the concrete wall with the agility of a cheetah chasing its prey, and headed in the opposite direction to where voices were heard, praying I would not be seen.

Of a quiet evening, on the incoming tide, I listened to the gentle splash of the waves as they touched the shoreline. Some of my friends and I sat on the concrete seawall and lingered after dusk, hoping to catch a glimpse of the black porpoises that swam in sequence to the fall of the waves. The noisy gulls, perhaps too exhausted from the day's squawking, settled down in their habitat and were not seen or heard of until the early hours next morning.

Children from different schools shared the large canteen for meals. At the end of the day, we played ball in the wide open fields. Evening concerts were held in the large community hall where the children sang hymns and songs in front of the seated clergy and the staff.

A slight breeze off the ocean caused the branches of the birch trees standing tall in the fields to sway gently, as the sun glistened on their silvery bark. My imagination, forever running wild, held my vision of little girls dancing to the music of the minuet. I strolled across the open fields and held my breath as I listened to the sound of a swish that caused me to look up then crouch down on the grass, as a football landed near my feet. In utter amazement, I picked up the football and cast my eyes round the field to see where it came from. In the distance a young boy wearing grey shorts and a white shirt walked with great strides toward me. I could not believe my eyes. *That* boy again!

Staring at him, I handed back the ball. As he turned to walk away I muttered, 'What a rude boy.' He didn't even say 'thank you.'

I then ran and ran across the playing fields, jumped the concrete steps leading down to the sandy shore, without as much as a look back!

That second encounter between a young girl and a boy during the hot summer month of July, little were they to realize the events yet to unfold when, years later, the girl began her lifelong researching the family's history and the boy also began searching for his roots.

Every year a social dance was held in the large school hall mid-July, for "old" girls and boys from the Kent area. My sister Elizabeth and I attended these functions in the hope of meeting up with past friends. On this particular occasion we arrived at the hall early, to the chatter of people inside. Entering through the school door we spotted a couple of our friends laughing to each other, as though their heads might drop off. We walked up to the chairs in which they sat – 'What's the joke?' we asked.

'Oh, it's her sex drive that sets her off,' said our friend Madeline, who still sported childhood freckles on her face, and was full of undulated mirth.

Although I was dying to hear the details, 'Let's leave it at that, shall we?' I suggested. 'We're in the presence of the holier than thou.'

Before there was sufficient time to catch up with our news, the door of the school hall suddenly swung open, causing a draft of air to waft in the room. In walked a stranger. No one took the slightest notice of him.

A slim, young man with black hair slicked well back over his forehead, and dark brown eyes, looked around the room before he swaggered nonchalantly across the floor, as though directed by some terrestrial light, and came to where Elizabeth and I sat.

After asking me if I would like to dance, 'Perhaps next time,' I said, with an uninterested look on my face.

Without further ado he took hold of Elizabeth's arm, saying, 'Come on, then, let's dance.'

She was flabbergasted! The look of surprise on the rest of our faces was enough to strike one dead. Elizabeth's countenance was one of horror! Dancing was not one of her fortes. She preferred to tuck her nose in a book: find a peaceful spot to sit in a corner of a large library, oblivious to the noise around her, and read to her heart's content. Her knowledge on many subjects became a topic of interest to family and friends who hoped one day, she might become an English teacher.

A young girl in her teens stood by a long table, busily taking charge of an old Victorian gramophone. As each record finished playing, with careful hands, she took it off the turning wheel and replaced it with another. Peering down to see it was safely in place, with her right hand she lifted the head holding a pointed needle and gently laid it on the record.

I watched with interest as my sister and the stranger danced to the tune of a waltz. Each time they glided past to where I sat with my friends, a smirk appeared on his face as he stared at me. At first I found this amusing but after several attempts to catch my eye, I decided enough was enough and decided not give him the satisfaction of knowing the game he was playing.

When the dance finished Elizabeth introduced the stranger to me saying, 'His name is William.'

Nodding my head, 'Not from this area, are you?' I queried.

'No, but I was brought up in another part of Kent.'

His eyes continued to study my face, as though searching a past recognition. Seeing the conversation went no further, he muttered something that sounded like, 'See you.'

We watched as he sauntered over to a girl seated alone, and asked her to dance.

'What do you make of that?' piped up one of our friends. 'And why did he keep looking at you, Caroline, with his dark brown eyes?'

'Can't imagine,' I briskly replied, in all innocence.

I wanted to drop the subject. Yet something niggled at the back of my mind and caused me to ponder: where, when, why?

Had we met during our school days? I shrugged off the thought. It must have been a dream.

The music suddenly stopped playing. One of the organizers held up her right arm and announced in a clear voice, 'Everyone is welcome to refreshments on the white-clothed table, at the top of the hall.'

We four friends strolled leisurely to the table where mounds of food stood on large china dishes, and piled our plates with a selection of sandwiches and small cakes, daring not to commit a mortal sin by wasting any of it. I was about to bite into a sandwich, when my sister nudged my elbow.

'Look, there's a huge iced chocolate cake in the centre of the table,' she bubbled. With her sweet tooth, I knew it wouldn't take her long to tuck into a large slice of it.

DISCHARGED OUT INTO THE WORLD

William Marshall had been raised at St. Mary's Orphanage in Gravesend, Kent. Upon reaching 16 years of age, the lads were typically placed on church-run farms as labourers, or shipped off to Canada or Australia to be indentured workers on farms and homesteads. In 1940, discharged from St. Mary's, 16-year-old William began his working life on a training farm at Bletchingly, Surrey. He found the work exceedingly boring, with no change from the rigid school discipline to life on the farm. His job was classified War Work. Any thoughts of escaping were tantamount to military leave without absence. The results of such actions, unthinkable! There could be no escaping. After two years working on the farm and having given what he thought his best endeavour to help in the war effort, each day he became more restless. He realized he did not want to be a farmer. He wasn't cut out to be one.

He rose early to bitterly cold winter mornings. Overnight frosts glistened on the barns and in the fields beyond, caused him to shiver and pull his jacket tighter round his thin body to keep warm. Each winter day seemed colder than the one before, and caused him to become more depressed. He simply hated this time of the year and saw not the beauty of the landscape, but the beast in it! To an artist, it would be paradise to

William, above, with friends at Bletchingly Farm, Surrey 1940.

perfect on canvas the silent countryside in its pristine white cloak, as icicles hanging on branches of the trees sparkled, enticingly, like crystal chandeliers.

Low temperatures kept the farm animals warming themselves inside the barns. Seemingly bored with not being able to stretch and graze outdoors, the cows made low bellowing sounds all hours of the day. Only the cats that prowled in and out of the property were oblivious to climatic conditions, with a liberty masking their faces.

William sat outside brooding on a bench as he looked at the landscape with a blank mind, occasionally being distracted when a hare twitching its nose, leaped and bounded inches away from him as though to tease: 'Try and catch me.'

In his troubled state of mind he was not about to fall flat on his face, trying to catch a silly hare. 'Either go back to your hole, or be caught and left hanging upside down outside a butcher's shop until you rot.'

His train of thought was suddenly distracted by the sound of horses' hooves crunching on the gravel path coming closer to him. Holding the reins in his hands, Jim, a lanky lad with a weather-beaten face and a mop of red hair, stopped the Clydesdale horse and cart in front of William.

'Come on then, time to work,' said Jim rubbing his cold hands. 'We've to haul hay in the cow's byres. Also collect eggs from the chicken coops.'

William looked at Jim, thinking wild horses would not drag him off the bench. But within seconds he took a running jump at the cart in an effort to get on, barely avoiding slipping on the ice as Jim held out his hand and pulled him on the wooden plank, to sit beside him. Offering him the reins and seeing the worried look on his friend's face, Jim laughed. 'Don't worry about guiding Old Ned. He knows the route inside and outside the farm, blindfold.'

Gingerly taking the reins from his friend, William held them between his closed knees and settled back on the hard seat, as Old Ned trotted at a leisurely pace toward the hayloft.

The next morning's early routine caused the riser to sniff the cold air, and collect his thoughts of the day's work ahead. William's future continued uppermost in his mind and he knew until the right path opened up it would dwell on him, like a festering boil. Animals were of no interest to him. He considered pigs dirty, snorting creatures who slopped about in mud. However, he gave second thought to the animal, considered it a necessary evil to provide food for the people, during this time of rationing.

Looking forlorn, his eyes travelling far beyond the meadows laced with overnight frost, when a familiar voice alerted his senses and caused him to sit upright on the outside bench. It was Jack, the local policeman, who stopped by with a mind of a good hot, strong cup of sweet tea and a chunk of fresh farmhouse bread.

A happy soul, always a permanent smile on his face, Jack saw both good and bad in the people he met regardless of their circumstances, be it related to a simple police matter or some misdemeanour requiring stronger action. Popular with his peers and the locals, Jack was recognized as a man who took his duties seriously. The school children begged the touch of his truncheon, held firmly behind his back.

William and Jack were soon to become good friends. On his off-duty time William spent it with Jack's family, who lived in the village of Bletchingly. Their close relationship sparked a new interest in William's life, to which he clung tenaciously.

The policeman, with ears bent, listened as William rambled non-stop about the workings on the farm, with less than a spark of enthusiasm. The local bobby knew as much if not more about what went on and how these raw recruits were treated, and boarded. Attentive to his friend's version of life aboard a farm, Jack sensed he was far from happy. But this was war! Did any person over the age of 16 years have a choice where to work, or the type of work they were ordered to do? This was a government-controlled era; to founder, listed you a deserter or one who failed to help their country in time of need.

'What's up, lad, did you lose a milk churn?' said Jack in a deep bass voice.

'Er, no, sir,' came the reply.

'Well, then, what's up with you?'

The policeman knew all the lads who came to work at the farm, then move on to greener pastures. Many stayed in touch with him after leaving the farm, and considered him to be their solid rock, a stepping stone from which to achieve future goals.

William made the effort to crease a smile on his face.

'It really isn't that bad once you get in the swing of things, is it, son?' said the policeman smiling, all the while swinging his truncheon from left to right behind his back.

Leaving William sitting on the bench with his thoughts, Jack entered the back door of the farmhouse through to the large white painted kitchen where the smell of fresh bacon, sausages and eggs were sizzling in a big black frying pan on top of the Argus stove. This was food at its best! The thought of downing a plateful caused him to salivate to the point fluid ran down the side of his mouth. The farmer's wife, Mavis, a short tubby person with a happy disposition who cooked for her family as well as for the lads who came to work on the farm, put a hot plate of food in front of him. At the ready, with knife and a fork in his hands, Jack tucked in.

As the months progressed, the friendship between farm trainee and the local bobby developed into a strong relationship. After weighing the pros and cons of learning how to run a farm and learning about far worse war work, William decided it wasn't that bad after all. One morning, as the two of them sat on a farm bench and watched ducks and chickens waddle off to a nearby field, then stop occasionally to peck for the choicest grub, William confided to the policeman he wanted to join the Navy. This was his ambition, and one he desperately wanted to achieve.

The policeman arched an inquiring eyebrow. 'Is that really what you want?'

'Yes,' came the fast response. 'It's been on my mind for a long time.'

'Well, if you're really serious we had better go to the nearest recruiting office on your next day off, where you can sign up.'

William's smile spread from ear to ear. On the appointed day, he stretched out on the seat beside Jack and watched the landscape, now green with the coming of spring, roll by. He felt the choice he made to join the Royal Navy was the right one. As they entered the village, Jack stopped the car and parked it outside the front of a large brick building.

Turning to William, he said, 'Well, lad, we've arrived. Let's get the formalities over with.'

Entering the building and seeing a young clerk sitting at the front desk, Jack inquired about a form to enlist in the armed forces. 'This lad's in a hurry to join up,' he said, all smiles.

Looking from one to the other and paying particular attention to the policeman's uniform, the clerk removed a form that sat in a tray on the top of his desk and handed it to William.

'Fill it in and bring it back to me,' said the clerk, with a curious look on his face, perhaps wondering if the lad accompanied by a policeman was in trouble and brought in to sign up, as retribution.

William gazed at the form. 'Oh, Lord,' he muttered, 'how on Earth am I going to fill in all the details when I don't even know the information they're asking?'

He looked at the form, as though willing his mind to surprise him by springing into action.

The policeman standing in the background, waited. Sensing his friend's anxiety, he walked over to the table where William sat, pen poised, his face a blank.

'Come on, lad,' urged the policeman, 'can't be all that bad, filling in a form. Give it here. Let's take a look at it?'

After scanning the form, a grin appeared on the policeman's face.

'Tell you what,' he advised. 'Fill in what you know. What you don't know, leave out.'

With the courage to write, William began to scribble in his personal details, occasionally stopping to look at Jack for guidance, then handed the form back to the desk clerk, half-completed.

'We'll notify you in due course,' said the clerk, with a less than interested look on his face as he took the application form from William and placed it back in the tray on top of his desk.

On the return journey Jack suggested to William it might be best if he didn't mention to the farmer his decision to leave the farm, or that he had applied to the Recruiting Officer at Godstone to join the Royal Navy.

'Wait,' he said, 'until you receive notification from the Enlistment office you have been accepted.'

'There will be plenty of other lads available for farm work to replace you,' he added.

William wasn't listening to what Jack had to say. He was too wrapped up with the idea of joining the Navy to take in the advice of his friend. The excitement of putting on a uniform was uppermost in his head. The day of reckoning could not come soon enough!

Grinning, he turned to Jack, and said, 'Great news, isn't it? I may get to sail the seven seas.'

'Better wait and see if you have been accepted and passed the medical exam,' the policeman cautioned.

Weeks went by, causing William to become nervous at the thought he may not get in. Finally, in the usual brown government envelope marked On His Majesty's Service, he received the news his application had been accepted, and was notified to undergo a medical examination within a week. After passing his medical with flying colours, he became a member of the armed forces.

After saying goodbye to his friends at the farm, and a fond farewell to the farmer's wife who fed him the best of food, William and Jack left by car to the railway station at Godstone, Surrey. As he was about to step on the train Jack held his arm, wished his friend the 'best of luck,' and slid a five pound note in his hand.

'You will write and let us know how you get on, won't you?'

Overwhelmed by the policeman's generosity, with a firm handshake and final farewell, William entered the carriage. Putting his bag in the rack overhead, he slid up the window of the carriage to get a last look at Jack standing on the platform, waving his arm, until the train disappeared out of sight along the tracks.

NAVY BLUE

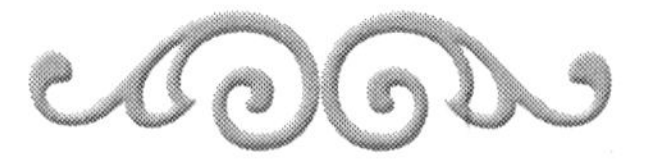

Joining the Royal Navy opened up new territories for William. Seafaring into foreign ports, he exuded energy in his new life, albeit at the bottom of the rung and subject to severe naval discipline.

Firmly developing his sea legs, throwing caution to the wind, and despite oft times he was forced to heave up overboard, he took to smoking and inhaling great gulps of nicotine as well as downing pints of beer and his quota of rum. During this time, as a raw recruit, his mates who were not short in coming forward to warn him of the sharks that lurked deep within the ocean bed, should he imbibe too much of the good stuff and find himself flung overboard.

'You definitely would not want to find yourself in those waters like an inebriated monkey, unable to climb back on board!' they chortled.

As he listened to the raucous cries of herring gulls circling the ship's mast, he pondered the fact he was unable to swim when he joined the service, but felt it held no deterrent to what he anticipated would be an interesting and worldly life.

With the essence of exuberance to leave well behind his behavioural childhood upbringing in the county of Kent, where the principles of curriculum were accuracy and pronunciation of words, William stripped this veil of his past to the bare bones when he became a rating of His

Majesty's Royal Navy. From now on, he deemed to choose the path of his lifestyle, and live to the very limit! Like a tiger let loose from its cage, to an unknown freedom, nothing was going to stop him from indulging in his new world. Only years later did he fully comprehend that the privilege of wearing the uniform of the Royal Navy demanded full respect to his King and country. Much to his chagrin, his wild shore excursions were to rebound on him. Not once, but twice.

Years later when Elizabeth and I visited William at his home near Portsmouth, Hampshire, we sat in armchairs in the living room, chatting our heads off! Listening to his rendition of what went on between himself and his mates who worked in the ship's engine room, we were aghast to hear of some of their escapades, and wondered how they managed to avoid being put on charge.

'It would not have surprised me at all,' I chirped, 'if the Captain tossed the lot of you overboard, to sink or swim among the man-eating sharks below.'

Elizabeth sat smiling, both hands folded in her lap. Perhaps she was thinking it was nothing more than hot air between raw recruits, who needed to blow off steam to strengthen themselves for whatever unforeseen challenges lie ahead.

With the war raging on different continents, reprisals, though minimized, were maintained strictly to Naval standards, to ensure the captain was not putting his ship in danger of capsizing.

Life on the ocean waves had its ups and downs for William, literally and figuratively. A fast learner, little escaped his quick mind as he progressively made his way from the bottom of the rung to a top level, dealing with the mechanics in the engine room. With a characteristic urge to turn the world upside down, slowly, he enjoyed what life had to offer, war or otherwise. Finally, he had found his niche.

Throughout his initial four years of Navy service, William did not go overseas. He remained at home shore bases, learning the mechanics and the running of the ship's engines. His natural talent and interest in this field of work enticed him to take as many engineering courses as allowed. From this vantage point, his character dramatically changed. No longer was he required to watch his P's and Q's. He developed a camaraderie with his mates, who were mainly born and bred in the East End of London. Working alongside them he picked up their Cockney accents with relish, and mimicked their every word. His mannerism changed with a view if he behaved and spoke like them, they would accept him. This lifestyle of work, fun and play appealed to his outgoing nature, but often led him to question the repercussions to follow.

On his first shore leave William, wearing bell bottom trousers and a Navy blue hat slung precariously at the back of his head, developed a character his sisters did not recognize in him as the stranger they met, unknowingly, for the first time at a school dance reunion.

He developed what is termed a Cockney swagger, causing his wide trouser bottoms to swing from side to side as he pushed his body in and out of pubs. Swinging through the doors, locals from inside the pub watched with curious eyes as they kept on drinking, while feeling the draft of energy exuded as he entered. His disregard of the English language noticeably changed, although he was careful not to drop his "aitches". Greeting a friend resulted with a slap on his back, 'Watcha, mate,' as he laughed his head off! You would have thought he hadn't seen his friend in months the way he greeted him, when it was only a matter of days.

Foreign expressions oozed from his mouth. Those closest to him looked nonplussed as they waited to hear what exactly he was trying to convey. A cigarette dangled permanently from his lips, causing reams of smoke to swirl upward, enough to make one cough and splutter. His sisters wondered if their new-found brother would ever be normal again. Despite encouraging him to think differently he revelled in the Cockney dialect as though he'd been born and bred within the sound of Bow Bells, and it remained with him to the end.

'Ain't life great?' he'd happily chuckle His bell bottoms swinging in unison from side to side as if ready to take flight, as he jingled and jangled shillings and pennies in his trouser pockets.

There was no stopping him! He flouted rules with careless rapture, but cautiously stayed within the radius of naval regulations. Shore leaves were spent in pubs and dance halls, and he never stopped hoping while winking at the girls for a dance. I was sure that one day he would come unstuck, or a girl would clout him round the ear for being cheeky, but it never happened.

He stepped out of being one character, working on the farm, and developed another when joining the Navy. This allowable freedom caused him to go from pious behaviour, to the utmost extreme. Carefree, he "threw caution to the wind" on shore leave, though consciously aware certain responsibilities were to be upheld at sea. His character never changed as he focused on doing what he considered the right thing, in each situation, at least by naval standards.

On one voyage, when a fire broke out in the engine room which could have destroyed his ship, William acted swiftly in getting the blaze under control, and was awarded a medal for bravery. From that moment on he began the climb up the career ladder, to further responsibilities.

TYING THE KNOT

A shy young girl named Violet, slim, with shoulder length black curly hair and a fresh complexion, regularly went to a dance hall in Walton-on-Thames, Surrey. On Saturday nights, the local girls partnered British, Canadian and American servicemen and jitterbugged to the loud music of a small band. This band was owned by a sleazy character named Eric Lawson, born and bred in the same town, who hit on the idea of running dances Friday, Saturday and Sunday nights. Money poured in to his coffers – not only did he pack the dance hall to capacity, but he also sold cheese and tomato sandwiches and refreshments at an exorbitant price. Alcohol was not permitted on the premises.

Below the dance hall, a British government restaurant served meals to the public for one shilling and sixpence. Although the main course was sparse, due to wartime rationing, the meals included desserts ranging from watery rice pudding, jam roly-poly with a custard sauce, far removed from the original thick custard, and a suet pudding with currents known as Spotted Dick.

The restaurant had once been a gentlemen's outfitter shop. It was confiscated by the government throughout the war and although it fed the public in general, the initial idea was to ensure factory workers, who toiled many long hours on production of vital components for military equipment, received a certain amount of nourishment to sustain them.

The dancers were barely able to navigate their partners across the floor, due to tight spaces, and made every effort to avoid crashing into each other or from hitting the four tall columns that held up the roof of the hall, as they swirled around the floor.

When the band played the jitterbug or the tango, it was every dancer for him or herself in performing intricate steps without banging into walls, or other partners. Finding space to dance became the butt of ongoing jokes! With a war brewing the young people inside the half-a-crown hop, as it became known, were intent on having a good time, as incendiary bombs droned their destruction elsewhere.

As though mesmerized by a magnet waving its energy to where William stood inside the door sizing up the evening's prospects, Violet caught his eye. She saw his Navy hat held at a spiffy angle, on the back of his head. A shy person, she cast her eyes sideways and continued to watch the dancers.

Suddenly a tap on her shoulder caused her to turn round, when a voice asked, 'Care to dance?'

She look up at the face of a sailor, and smiled. Before the words came out of her mouth, she found herself caught up in his arms. While they danced Violet felt he was holding her tighter than necessary. He chatted, and laughed, as though life was a "bed of roses". The war did not enter his head as he continued to clasp his partner firmly by the waist, and enjoy each minute.

'Where do you live?' came his usual line of questioning. 'Come often, do you?'

Violet barely rose her head to his questions, which came faster than she could answer, as his arm continued its grip around her waist. As they danced, she gave him her best smile. William had never before danced with a partner who didn't want to talk about all and sundry, as they glided across the floor. This girl spoke not a word. She acknowledged his questions by moving her head up and down. A timid person, who at best kept to herself, she was not comfortable speaking about her personal life when meeting a stranger. Particularly sailors, whose one intent was to enjoy shore leave dancing when his sea legs were on dry land.

Preparing to leave, she stopped by the cloakroom to pick up her coat and recognized the voice from behind ask, 'Can I see you home?'

Seeing it was the sailor with whom she danced, while he chatted up a storm, she agreed.

For the remainder of his shore leave William and Violet dated, danced, hired a punt on the River Thames, stopping at a nearby pub for lunch and cold drinks. When asked, Violet agreed to be his girlfriend.

He was in cloud nine! 'Will you write to me?' he said in a flurry of words.

Throughout their time spent together, Violet fed him snippets of news about her family. She gradually gained more confidence speaking to this new boyfriend, who gave her the impression he had not a care in the world. Shyly she told him that, at an early age, her elder sister and herself were adopted.

Could this have been the vibe that drew them together in the dance hall? As neither one were brought up in a biological family environment?

Violet's adoptive parents never divulged to her or her sister the identity of their real parents and why they were adopted, or from where their family originated. A dark secret throughout their childhood, they never questioned the reason how this kind and caring couple in their late fifties came to accept them.

Their "father", a tall slim man with a slight bent, was employed in the parks department in the town of Kingston-on-Thames. A well-known horticulturist, he often gave lectures at the famous Kew Gardens in Surrey.

When Violet introduced William to her father, his deep blue eyes questioned the sailor about his family background. Explaining simply as possible, William said he was put in care at an early age but unable to give him the reason. When he reached the age of sixteen he was given the choice to begin his adult life, either emigrate to Canada or Australia, or work on a farm.

Nodding at William, the old man could hardly contain his curiosity. In his right hand, he picked up a briar-wood pipe. With his left hand he stuffed the small bowl with an evil-smelling tobacco, and put the pipe in his mouth. His upper lip showed a deep yellow stain from constant smoking. Puffing, without taking a breath, heavy smoke permeated the room and wafted upward to the ceiling.

Staring William in the face, 'Ever know your parents?', he bluntly asked.

'No,' William replied, shifting his body awkwardly, crossing one leg over the next.

For once in his life, he remained silent, lost for words. 'How can I respond to past history when I don't even know it myself?' he muttered.

This caused the listener to straighten his back up in the chair, puff harder on his pipe, all the time arching dark bushy eyebrows up and down. The creases on his forehead ran deep from the bony ridge over the eyes to the hairline. Looking at this formidable stranger who sat too close for comfort, William studied the dark expression on his inquisitor's face.

Perhaps thinking what William was thinking, the man peered closer. 'Well, looks as though you two were meant to meet, being more or less in dire circumstances and put in different homes,' was his casual remark.

The inquisition over! Having lost interest in a conversation seemingly going nowhere, the old man eased himself from the chair and went in the garden.

As though propelled by a tidal wave, William and Violet spent the rest of his shore leave together. Taking the "bull by the horn" he set out to enjoy every second of his leave knowing at any time he could be called back to duty, posted to heavens know where!

Going back over the years I often wonder how two people so different in character could get on so famously, and tie the knot. Young beautiful Violet, so shy. William, flamboyant with his never-ending jokes and zest for living, dared anyone to challenge him when having a good time on shore leave or in the pubs. A gregarious character unto himself. Somehow, life for them worked, no holds barred.

In 1946, their marriage vows were taken at the Kingston Registry Office, with Violet's sister and adoptive parents in attendance. After the ceremony, the couple left for London and spent their honeymoon at the servicemen's club in Waterloo. All too soon William returned to duty at his shore base, Portsmouth. Violet went home to her family at Cheam.

On shore leaves, William stayed with his wife in the family home. Often they took bus rides to Kingston, hopping off the bus halfway at Hampton Court, where the public are allowed in the palace grounds. The intricate maze and pathways in the gardens caused many unwary visitors much concern as they tried to extricate themselves in and out of the maze, only to find themselves hopelessly lost until another visitor came upon the scene, and guided them on the right path. Some visitors took the plunge going in the maze, once. The second time seemed too adventurous. Often it led to a frightening experience when people found they were lost. It caused more anxiety to know the garden gates were always locked after visiting hours, and palace staff did not search the grounds for dawdling visitors!

At that time I was living in a house in Walton-on-Thames, not far from Kingston. On a bitterly cold evening in December, a loud knock on the front door caused me to hurry downstairs and open it. A man stood on the doorstep, shivering, with a wide grin on his face.

Before I could open my mouth he bubbled, 'Remember me? I'm your brother William.'

I invited him in. When I last saw this fellow it was at a school reunion dance Elizabeth and I attended. We were both in our teens. At the time, although strange thoughts filtered in my head half-recognizing her dance partner, I had not connected his "Cockney swagger" to the 10-year-old boy at the holiday camp at Dymchurch, Kent. But now, here was that young lad, now a grown man standing in my hallway.

'How did you know where I lived?' I asked.

He'd been to St. Anne's school in Orpington and one of the nuns gave him my address.

Although our first meeting as adults was a little restrained, we promised to stay in touch. A few weeks later, I met William in Kingston. It was there he introduced his wife Violet to me. We took to each other immediately.

From then on, I frequently met up with William and Violet to go in a local pub for cold drinks, and a chat. Violet and I were non-drinkers. The urge to indulge in anything stronger did not appeal to either of us until in later years we succumbed.

William's four years service in the Navy did not require him to undertake active duty overseas though he was stationed at shore bases at Chatham, Portsmouth, Lowestoft near Great Yarmouth and other ports round the English Channel. Thus week-end passes made it possible for him to spend as much time as possible with his wife.

In 1947, his service with the Navy ended. After signing his release papers, with two of his mates also released from duty, they headed to a pub in Portsmouth. The three sat on stools close to the bar counter and as they drank from pint glasses, commiserated to each other how they would fare and the directions their lives would take. Leaving the pub to catch trains to London, the three shook hands and made a pact to stay in touch.

Initially, after he was discharged, it pleased William to be home. However a few months after being on dry land, he found civilian life a different "kettle of fish", as he was now required to support not only himself but also his family. The past four years the Navy took care of his daily needs and caused him little thought or concern about his welfare.

Having acquired good skills as a mechanical engineer during his service, and taking many exams to extend his knowledge and career, did not necessarily give his qualifications an "edge" above all others, when searching for work. Nevertheless, for one so gregarious in nature it came as a shock "out of the blue" when he realized for all his efforts to find a job there were none for the taking, let alone the pickings.

Checking the local engineering companies he applied for one job after the other, only to find positions were few and far between. This turn of event caused him to realize how fortunate he had been to serve in His Majesty's Royal Navy without worrying where his next meal came from, plus the joy of jingling shillings and sixpences in his bell bottom trouser pockets with a view the flow of money would last forever. It was a rude awakening when finding himself in this position, knowing companies were no longer hiring now government contracts had ceased since the war ended. Any chances of future work appeared exceedingly slim.

It was during this time of financial crisis that Violet found herself pregnant with their first child. William was consciously aware of the fact that without an income he would be unable to support her or their forthcoming child. Putting his arm round her shoulders, as though to reassure her, he announced, 'The only way I'm able to deal with our money problems is to rejoin the Navy.'

'But, you've only just come out of the Navy,' said Violet, her mouth pinched in a stubborn line. 'I'm sure something will turn up. Give it another try.'

With employment at a standstill, William knew in his heart anyone who was searching for work may have to wait for months perhaps years, until companies were able to increase their book orders and hire additional staff. It was a difficult decision whether to appease his wife to remain in civilian life or rejoin the service. Gently lifting up Violet's face he looked compassionately in her eyes, wishing for a miracle to happen.

'There's little chance of a job now the factories continue to lay people off, instead of hiring,' he told her, trying his best to convince her it was not a question of choice where he worked. The criteria was money, and enough to pay the bills. Looking at him with an urgency in her voice, Violet insisted he keep on trying.

A shadow of depression hung over the young couple. Sitting together in the deep couch in her parent's living room, silent in thought, they knew life would be a struggle without a steady income. The weeks dragged by. Each day William nervously watched as his saved Navy pay dwindled, to a point they would soon be penniless. If he didn't find work before his money ran out, the consequences of not being able to provide a decent home for Violet now pregnant, would be too awful to bear. As her pregnancy progressed, she knew her days working at the office were soon to end. One path Violet was determined not to follow under any circumstance, was to go into debt.

Searching William's face, whose mind appeared elsewhere, she finally said, 'If this is the answer to our financial problems, then you must go!' Violet relented, in a voice barely audible. To her, it was the final assault on what should be a normal family life, both parents sharing the joy of seeing their family grow.

In the same year 1947 he was discharged, William rejoined the Royal Navy. Throughout the years when back in service, he sailed the high seas to foreign ports. Life for him would never be the same.

With William back in the uniform Violet did not expect to face another dilemma, now the monetary one had been resolved. When she told her adoptive parents of her pregnancy, they greeted the news with joy. Congratulations were freely bestowed. A few days after, and the excitement of the moment had settled down, her parents advised there was insufficient room in the house to accommodate a baby and she would have to find a place elsewhere to live. This came as a shock to gentle Violet who accepted life for what it offered, good or bad. The mere thought of having to undertake this task in finding accommodation for herself and unborn child without the help of William, caused her to worry about the outcome.

The housing shortage was at its worse level since the war and the prospects of finding anything remotely suitable was virtually impossible. Tears threatened to fall down Violet's face. She sat on the edge of her bed nervously twisting her fingers. Hearing a gentle knock on the door she gulped back tears that threatened to pour down her face, as her elder sister Mabel entered the bedroom. Seeing the sad look on Violet's face she went over to the bed and put an arm round her shoulders. The news that her sister could not stay in the house, due to lack of accommodation for the baby, was the reason their parents asked her to leave, Mabel quietly reiterated.

'We will search the neighbourhood together. Failing that, we can go into Kingston where there may be a better chance of finding a room,' Mabel said, trying to cheer her.

On a freezing cold November afternoon, the two sisters decided to brave the elements and go house-hunting. Wearing long brown woollen overcoats and matching colour hats, as they opened the front door to the house a gust of wind caused them to gasp for breath, and hold on tight to their hats. Gingerly, closing the front door behind them, they made their way down the concrete steps to the pavement below.

The tall silver birch trees standing on either side of the wide avenue reached skyward. Strong winds forced their delicate branches to swing dangerously, as though ready to snap. Taking in deep gulps of fresh air, and to avoid slipping on wet leaves on the damp ground, the sisters held on tightly to each other as they made their way around the neighbouring avenues. Clutching the collars of their winter coats high up to their cheeks to keep warm, they checked the front gardens and screened with sharp eyes for possible rental signs in windows. None were to be seen.

Tugging on the sleeve of her sister's coat, Violet pointed skyward. Looking at the black clouds, 'it's going to rain buckets,' she said.

Mabel sensed the oncoming rain and decided they get back inside the house before the clouds burst, and soaked them. With red cheeks and cold noses they linked arms and headed for home, feeling despondent with their efforts, but a little wiser. Both agreed their decision to trudge the streets looking for rental signs on a freezing cold day, was not a good one.

As the months passed, the sisters became increasingly anxious when all their efforts to find alternative accommodation for mother and baby, had failed. 'Winter conditions are not a good time to be out in the streets,' said Mabel, who was concerned for her sister, now four months pregnant.

Violet had never been a robust person, and her lack of energy did not give her the strength to continue with the search for alternative accommodation. She shrugged her shoulders and said, 'What will be, will be,' and appeared in a blasé mood, which was totally uncharacteristic to her nature.

In April 1948, Violet entered the Kingston hospital and gave birth to a healthy son. The news reached William as his ship sailed into the Port of Malta.

Shortly after the birth of her son, Violet wasted little time in picking up copies of the local newspapers in and around Surrey. She did not wish to impose further on her adoptive parents, despite the assurance from Mabel they would not ask her to leave with a baby until other accommodation had been found. She was however determined to surge ahead.

Checking the newspaper columns she saw a room advertised for rent in Kingston-on-Thames, not far from Cheam where her family lived. Giving her sister the news, she asked if the baby could be left in her care while she was out searching the area. As fast as her legs could move, she took the bus from Cheam to Kingston. With the newspaper tucked safely under one arm, she hopped off the bus and walked within easy distance from the bus depot until she came to the front door of the address advertising a room for rent. She banged hard on the knocker. The door flew open, as though on a timer. Violet stood, paralyzed, and looked into the face of a scruffily-dressed woman, aged somewhere in her late forties, a cigarette dangling from her mouth. Her dingy yellow skin cried out for a good scrub of soap and water. Not to be put off by this unhealthy-looking individual Violet told her she had come about the room, advertised in the paper.

'Come on up,' said the smoker, trudging ahead of Violet up the narrow stairwell, to show her a small room that lacked the size of a mouse hole. A look of surprise appeared on Violet's face, as she entered. The room was simply furnished of non-descriptive colours, with the barest of furniture, but it was clean.

William, Malta 1954.

Walking over to the window, she looked down on one of the busiest streets in Kingston. Across from the other side of the street stood the gas works, with its tall black chimneys towering above. It was not a pretty sight; nevertheless, an essential one. The chimneys never stopped belching out gaseous fumes that caused even the healthiest of people to cough and choke. Specks of coal dust landed on the clothing of the unsuspected trespasser who sneaked into the yard after dark, hoping to pick up free bits of coal or coke without being seen. Often the local bobby, with his truncheon at the ready, stopped by the gas works to check for intruders. If caught, one found themselves standing before a local judge. Nicking coke or coal was considered a crime, with supplies still on ration, years after the Second World War.

'You can share the bathroom and kitchen, if you want,' said a breathless voice, choking on the cigarette.

Violet nodded. Did the woman assume the use of such facilities were unnecessary?

After inspecting the room, 'I'll take it,' Violet said in a timid voice.

'It's a month's rent in advance,' the smoker was quick to advise.

When Violet handed over the money and asked her new landlady for a receipt, she grasped the money from her, and gave a wide smile.

Boarding the bus to Cheam, Violet sat deep in thought. She wondered how William would react to the move to Kingston when he saw where his family lived, in a room barely big enough to attract the smallest of mice.

In the trunk of his car, Violet's father packed her few belongings. Mabel sat in the back seat of the car next to her sister, and held the baby in her lap. With the key given to her by her landlady, Violet opened the front door to the flat and went up the narrow stairwell to reach the rented room on the upper floor. Father and sister trailed behind, then left the luggage by the side of the small bed for Violet to unpack. Going down the same way they entered, the old man did not stop tut-tutting until he stepped down on the pavement outside the front door. Giving him a quizzical look Mabel took his arm and without a word spoken, sensing what was on her father's mind, she opened the side door of the car and stepped in.

Violet's new abode caused her to tramp up and down the narrow stairwell when she needed to go shopping. But she never complained. Her main concern was a roof over her head and that of her three-month-old son. She told herself she could manage the stairs between the pram and the shopping bags, and was totally convinced the opportunity to move into a larger place would arise in the not too distant future.

The building could not be classified luxurious, by any means of the imagination. It was in dire need of repairs and in the opinion of the owner, a waste of time and money to replace broken windows caused by continual bombing. It was a sorry sight. Seeing them boarded up with heavy cardboard the neighbours and renters went about shaking their heads, it being a lost cause to complain. They knew enough about the character of the owner, knowing he would be the last person to deal with a dysfunctional building, but it would not deter him from being first in line to make an early claim for damages to the British government when the war ended.

A family by the name of Dwyers rented the top floor of the building. By sub-letting a room they were able to get money to buy the extra bottle of stout and cigarettes. This affordable luxury appeared their sole pleasure in life. Originally from Birmingham, known for its metal foundries, 110 miles northwest of London, in the industrial Black Country, they moved to Kingston-upon-Thames in the mid- 1940s.

The husband, Eric, a tall skinny man with jet black hair and a complexion that would do justice to any prison pallor, had dark brown eyes. They were so deep, enough to remind one of the swarthy Romney gypsies who roamed the English countryside earlier than the 1920s. Convinced he was on par with tenor Donald Peers, a popular singer at that time in England, lustily he sang at the top of his voice. This caused his lungs to blow in and out, like a pair of bellows used to spark the flames with sticks and rolled-up newspaper, to light a fire.

'The whole place shakes, with his every rendition. If he had a softer voice, how nice for the baby to be lulled to sleep,' whispered Violet to William, on one shore leave.

Eric and his wife, Lil, pallid and haggard-looking from heavy smoking and late night drinking, sported deep black shadows beneath their puffy eyes. At our first meeting, although the variety of food was still restricted, Lil's enormous bodily weight took me by surprise. I thought, how can anyone be so fat when so little food is available? I then reasoned to myself, lots of people in England were forced to eke out their rations by buying extra supplies through the profitable black market.

Black marketeers were known to make sizeable fortunes, enough to retire to warmer climes after the war. That was one rumour in Walton-on-Thames about our local butcher. He took extra half crowns from his customers if a wink suggested to him that getting a spare lamb's kidney or a piece of beef suet, used for making roly-poly puddings and dumplings, was well worth paying the extra money.

This additional piece of ration-free contraband was tucked inside the newspaper when the butcher wrapped up a customer's weekly ration of meat, without asking for next week's meat ration coupon. How they came by this surplus of goodies was a mystery. No one, of course, dare utter a word for fear of someone standing close by had large, authoritative ears. Billboards around the neighbourhood showed a picture of a man pointing fingers outward, with the words coming out of his mouth: *Walls have ears!* Looking at these were enough to caution the most talkative of neighbours.

Rumours ran riot that some of the crates of food destined for delivery to various parts of the country conveniently fell off lorries. When the driver recovered the crates from the ground and deemed it spoiled, he dropped the load off at a specified food station where it was declared unfit for human consumption. The general public were not easily fooled when families of the drivers were generous to surreptitiously share the spoils with some of their neighbours. 'Mum,' being the adjective. It became an hilarious joke to those who survived, under stringent regulations. That so much, when so little was available, this could happen under the noses of authority, left one totally in the dark.

Violet named her baby Daniel. A happy child with sturdy legs, his black hair showed early signs of tight curls. I wasn't living that far from the family when William came home on leave, so I often visited. Violet was a caring mother. As I watched parent and child develop a closeness, I hoped somewhere along the years life would provide them a happy, contented future.

On shore leave, William spent his time with his wife and son in the small rented room on the top landing of the building, where at the other end of the landing, lived the Dwyers. During the time spent with them I never heard a complaint about their living conditions or whether William felt constrained in their cramped accommodation, after spending many months in the swells of open waters. He kept his thoughts to himself hoping one day better accommodation was on the horizon, and there would be a garden where his son would play.

It was a dreary dull morning, and feeling as gloomy as the dark clouds above, William casually strolled to the town of Portsmouth, his mind set on one thing. With downcast eyes, he suddenly came to a jolt as he collided with a person walking toward him. Looking up he was shocked to see it was his Chief Petty Officer whom he had forced off the pavement, and was now standing in the road.

Smartly saluting, 'Sorry, sir, didn't see you coming.'

The CPO stared at him. 'Looks as though you've come unstuck, somewhere, Marshall. Eyes up when you wear the King's uniform.'

'Yes, sir. Thinking of houses, sir,' William sheepishly grinned.

'Good luck, you'll need it. Like looking for an needle in a haystack, if you ask me,' said the CPO as he walked in the opposite direction toward the barracks, looking none the worse for being pushed in the road.

'That was a close one,' William said to himself, as he headed back to base.

The following week William and two of his mates were out searching for houses in the Cosham and Portsmouth area. Randy, in his early thirties with light brown hair and sparkling green eyes, came from the East End of London. With a carefree nature, on par with his two friends, he had few worries in the world to concern him. His friend Joe, of the same age, with black hair and eyes that penetrated one's soul when he looked at you, was somewhat in tune with William who loved laughing and joking. He was born and bred in the Hackney district of the East End, not far from where Randy lived.

Taking duty leave together, the three had but one train of thought uppermost on their mind: "Paint the town red", down pints of beer in pubs with nautical names, The Nelson, Ship's Inn, Mary Rose and others that boasted serving beer that was beer and not as a few publicans were known to do, water it down to increase their profit. Some publicans were of the opinion when a sailor had money in his pocket to burn and became drunk in the process, he neither cared nor realized the quality of beer he was drinking. It was an on-going motto with the three sailors: 'live for the day, tomorrow may be too late.'

Their plans to search the neighbourhood for accommodation they believed to be in good faith, but after walking several miles, our illustrious trio began to sag in the knees. Sweat oozed across their brows, and trickled down their shirt collars. William, generally known for his "happy-go-lucky" nature, looked as though life had dealt him a thundering blow! Noticing the look on his friend's face, Joe suggested they take a break and go to The Sailor's Arm pub in Portsmouth and cool off with a pint of beer, with every intent after resting and quenching their thirst, to plod on with the search.

In typical naval style, bell bottoms afloat, they sauntered through the swinging doors of the pub and looked for the nearest bar stools. Randy, placid and easy-going, surprised his friends by saying, 'We're probably wasting our time looking for something that's not there.' He seemed more anxious than anything to get his lips on a pint mug, rather than pound the streets looking for houses.

Sitting on a bar stool, Joe turned to William and asked, 'what'll you have, mate?'

'Oh, make mine a pint, with a chaser.' [Scotch whiskey]

'Same here,' Randy chirped.

'You will, will you,' came the reply. 'Fat chance on Navy pay.'

'Just joking, beer is fine,' the two said, holding tongues at the ready to quench their thirst.

Sitting on bar stools with pints in their hands, Randy and Joe commiserated over William's housing dilemma. As they downed one pint after the one, their concerns gradually faded into a misty euphoria. Taking extra care not to flip over the bar stools as they jumped off, the three left the pub singing happily on their way back to base.

The noise in the ship's engine room made it difficult for the sailors to hold a conversation. Hearing a thunderous order forced in his right ear, William held one hand over it, as he felt his feet rise from the floor. Turning round he looked into the face of his Chief Petty Officer and wondered if a reprimand was forthcoming due to arriving back at the barracks, slightly inebriated.

'Marshall,' said the voice, 'heard a house going for rent in Cosham. Go to it, when you're off duty.'

His hands covered in grease, William saluted, 'Thank you sir, thank you.'

When the officer disappeared within seconds of arriving and was out of sight, William hurried to where his mates were working to give them the news.

'What brought that on?' Randy cautiously queried. 'Unusual for CPO to bother with rating's personal matters.'

'No idea. What's more, I really don't care,' came William's fast response.

Two days after receiving the news, Randy, Joe and William caught a bus to Cosham, a stone's throw away from their shore base in Portsmouth, and arrived at the address written down on a piece of paper by the CPO.

Standing outside the empty semi-detached house they wondered how on earth to get in, without a key. Taking the initiative, William went to the front door of a neighbour's house and banged loudly on the knocker. A plump woman with long streaky ginger hair hanging over her shoulders who looked to be in her forties, gently opened the door. Eyes popping like corks, she viewed the sailors standing on her doorstep with grins on their faces, wide as chimps.

'Well, I never, the fleet has arrived,' she spluttered, holding her fat arms across her heavy breasts. 'What can I do for you good-looking sailors?' she pertly asked.

William studied the suspicious look on the woman's face and said to himself, 'Even if she has the key, she'll never give it to us.' But he was not to be fobbed off!

'Do you have the key to the house next door?' William asked.

'As a matter of fact, I do. The owner leaves it in my care.'

Not wishing to lose a minute, William told the woman he was given to understand the house was for rent, and he needed the front door key to get in.

As though sensing the urgency of the sailors' visit, 'Well, far as I know,' she blurted, 'the owner does want to rent it.'

Without another word she disappeared inside her house, leaving the door slightly ajar.

'What do you make of that?' asked Randy. 'Bit of a queer one, if you ask me.'

The sailors stood patiently waiting on the doorstep, and were curious to know what sort of house this woman lived in. Before getting a chance to step over the threshold to peek inside, the woman came out of her door with the key in her left hand and handed it to William. Giving her a wide smile, he thanked her.

'Mind you bring it back,' she said, with a gleam in her eyes.

Before she could utter another word of advice, Joe urged his friends, 'Come on mates, can't waste any more time. Let's go and take a look inside,'

Cautiously inserting the key inside the lock of the front door, William opened it for them to enter. Nostrils began to twitch as the musty smell inside made all three want to sneeze.

'Gawd,' said Joe holding a finger to his nose. 'This place smells like Billingsgate fish market. What it needs is a bit of good salt air.'

Taking hold of the latches, he threw open all the windows.

'That's better,' he laughed, as his nose continued to twitch.

The front door of the house led into a narrow passage at the end of which was the sitting and dining-cum-kitchen. From this area, French doors opened out onto a small garden with enough space to grow vegetables, and a spot for William's son to play.

Leading from the front door, a staircase went up to the top floor with three bedrooms and a small bathroom which included a toilet. Taking note of everything, with future prospects of purchasing the house when he left the service, William could not believe his stroke of good luck!

Going from room to room he hummed, mentally planning what a coat of paint here and there would do to make the walls look cleaner and fresher. With his head in the clouds, and mind set, once the family moved in the house he would "dolly up" the place. Little did he envisage his days at Portsmouth were numbered. Overseas duty was about to be called.

Noting his mates were busy exploring and checking the bare floor boards downstairs for termites or dry rot, he ambled over to them. 'Anything foreign down there?' he questioned.

'No, nothing here to worry about,' chuckled Randy.

All three took a second look round the house, and nodded approval. Saying, 'it's got possibilities after a good scrub and clean-up,' William closed and locked the front door.

He held the key in his right hand. With his left hand holding on to the knocker of the neighbour's front door, he was about to bang on it when immediately, the door flew open! The woman with long streaky ginger hair stood inside. She gazed hard at the three sailors, standing near her doorstep.

William handed back the key to her and rubbing his hands together, laughed, 'Won't be long before I'll need it again.'

The woman moved to get a closer look at the sailors at though she had something else on her mind. 'Well, lads, see you sooner than later,' she cried, giving them a wicked wink.

George West was a stocky man with a ruddy complexion, who came from a small farming community near the dales of Yorkshire. Throughout the war he felt duty-bound to help a serving sailor in His Majesty's Royal Navy. Albeit, with strong leanings toward assisting him spend his service money which, in his opinion, was money wisely spent.

William, and his two mates Randy and Joe, who tagged along for the ride, went to see Mr. West where he lived on the outskirts of Portsmouth. When the sailors arrived on his doorstep, with the aplomb of entertaining royalty, he invited them inside to his well-furnished living room. Pointing to Chippendale wing-back chairs, he offered them a seat. Seeing they were comfortably seated and had his full attention, Mr. West asked if they would like a drink. The minute he left the room, the sailors chatted without a pause as they pointed with fingers at the fine pieces of antique furniture.

'Well,' Joe whispered, 'he's not short of money with this lot. Just look at it. Must have cost a fortune.'

When Mr. West returned to the living room holding a tray of glasses with lemonade, the sailors were back in their seats and accepted with alacrity the glasses handed to them.

William was eager to achieve a done deal to rent the house in Cosham as soon as possible. The three were shortly due back at base and he didn't want to miss other plans they had made ahead of time for the evening's entertainment. Mr. West however did not appear to be in any hurry to negotiate and listening to all his humming and haggling, William thought he'd burst a blood vessel. But he was not prepared to leave until they had amicably agreed on the rent.

Randy and Joe patiently sat waiting for landlord and sailor to come to a compromise. Knowing William was not going to budge on what he considered a fair price, Mr. West finally succumbed and the two signed an agreement. Shaking hands with Mr. West whose face was now beet red from using up too much energy, William gave him a wide smile. Looking at his new landlord's countenance, William sensed he was as pleased to finally find a tenant capable of paying the monthly rent. It didn't concern him that on-going raids in the area, at any time, could demolish his property. He wanted money now, and not wait to negotiate with a government who appeared to all intents and purposes a bit on the stingy side when it came to reimbursing the owners of war property damages.

As William was about to leave with his friends, Mr. West inquired, 'You know where to find the house key, don't you, lad?'

William nodded. 'Okay if I paint up the house a bit?'

'Of course, lad,' replied Mr. West, enthusiastically, excited at the thought of seeing new paint inside and outside the house, in the hope it increased the value of his property. 'I'm sure you'll do a good job with the help of your pals,' he added.

'Next time you're on leave, look me up. You and your friends can meet me for a few pints in the local.'

Paying Mr. West his month's rent in advance, William left with his companions, jingling the few coins he had left in his trouser pocket. Chatting non-stop, they returned to Portsmouth and on the way popped in for a quickie at the local pub, excited as school boys on a sports outing, before heading back to base.

William decided he would not give Violet the good news he had rented a house in Cosham until it was squeaky clean and freshly-coated with paint. Randy and Joe helped willingly with the painting but were to constantly remind him, 'you owe us.'

On a hot summer day in August and a clear blue sky, the three sailors stood outside the barrack gates. Tall beech trees lined the entrance to the base, and a gentle breeze off the ocean caused the branches on the trees to sway in rhythmic motion. With noses held skyward, our three friends inhaled the salty sea air. 'Smells so good,' remarked Joe. 'Enough to make one want to drink it.'

Randy and William looked at one another and couldn't believe what they had just heard. Joe getting all sloppy about wanting to drink salty sea air. 'Me thinks,' said Randy peering closer at Joe, 'you need a stiff one.'

William's request for compassionate leave was granted to allow him move his family from Kingston-upon-Thames, Surrey to their new home at Cosham. The three walked in step with each other as they left the barracks and headed toward the railway station to catch the train to Kingston. The southbound train from Portsmouth slowly chugged its way out of the station on command of the tubby porter wearing a black peaked cap who blew sharply on his whistle, while waving his green flag.

As they settled down in the seats inside a third class carriage, the sailors chatted humorously, while slyly giving the eye to other travellers. No girls aboard today. Just the elderly chancing a day's outing to get them wherever they were going, in one piece. Before the sailors were aware they had arrived at their destination, carriage doors were flung open and passengers scurried toward the exit.

'Why all the rush?' asked Randy.

Cigarettes dangling from their mouths and bell bottoms swinging at a leisurely pace, the sailors reached the porter standing at the gate and handed him their railway passes. Looking at all three, the porter grinned, 'Have a good time, lads,' thinking all sailors came to Kingston for one reason, to "paint the town red".

'Sure will, mate,' all three responded, laughing.

The porter shook his head.

Violet's place of accommodation was a short distance from the railway station and with the help of Randy and Joe, William was able to pack her few belongings within less time than it took for them to walk from the railway station to where she lived on Richmond Road.

The Dwyers stood on the top landing, puffing on cigarettes, all the while casting wary eyes on the sailors as they packed the suitcases. When they were ready to leave Eric cocked his head toward Violet and said to no one in particular, 'She's the best renter we've ever had. We're sorry to see her go. So quiet, we hardly knew a baby was in the flat.'

Looking at Eric and Lil, Violet thanked them.

'Come back and see us, won't you?' they chortled, as the cigarettes held between their lips caused ash to fall to the floor each time they spoke.

Smiling, she carried Daniel, now fifteen months old, in her arms, and held on tight to William as they descended the narrow staircase. Randy and Joe following behind with the suitcases.

Once out on the street pavement William took in a deep breath, looked up at the sky, as though in prayer. 'Thank the good Lord that's over,' with ne'er a thought of gazing back as they headed toward the railway station to catch the return train to Portsmouth.

William's Navy pay was stretched to the point it did not allow him an opulent lifestyle. He was after all in His Majesty's service, classified as a rating, and did not have the right to provoke the issue of earning more pay unless recognized by his superior officers that his engineering skills deemed him sufficiently well qualified for an increase. However, it was not beyond his powers to make use of his earnings to help with his family's small comforts. When they arrived back at Portsmouth railway station, Randy and Joe returned to base saying, 'See you later.'

Seeing a taxi pull up outside the station William stretched out his right arm, 'Can you take us to Cosham?' he asked the driver.

When they arrived at the front door of a semi-detached house William took a key from his pocket, unlocked the door, and ushered Violet inside. He put down the suitcases, then took his son from the arms of his mother. Violet walked slowly along the narrow hall from the front door as though on an exploration hunt, while sniffing the freshly-coated paint, hoping the smell from it would dissipate with time for the sake of her baby. Going into the living room she took a good look round and noticed it was sparsely furnished, with second-hand furniture. Seeing the disappointed look on her face William explained that he and his mates had bartered with a local dealer to buy the best pieces of furniture for sale, at the best price, including free delivery.

'That is really all I can afford at this time,' he said, feel slightly humbled.

Not wishing to appear ungrateful for his efforts to find her and her son a home, Violet shyly went over to him and planted a kiss on his cheek. Inspecting the living room further she noticed a small fireplace with marble-tiles surrounding it, in the centre wall. This appeared to be their only source to heat the house. The heavy black iron grate in the fireplace, orange with rust, looked as though it would disintegrate if anyone was foolish enough to try picking it up.

'Where on Earth am I going to get the coal to put in the fireplace?' she asked herself.

The upper floor of the house took on a new dimension to the new tenant. As Violet climbed the stairs her fingers touched the hairline cracks and small holes in the walls that were badly in need of repair, and cried out for a fresh coat of paint. If her husband was unable to do these repairs, she decided she would tackle the job herself.

Known as the "box" room, which is much smaller than the other two bedrooms, she chose this one for her baby son. Walking to the end of the landing she opened the door to the bathroom and toilet, peered inside, and paused. She imagined having a luxurious bath in the scented crystals William brought back from the Orient, and not having to breath in the smell of heavy cigarette smoke that hung in the Dwyer's bathroom. It caused her to smile, as she quietly closed the door.

William's compassionate leave ended all too soon. He returned to shore base at Portsmouth feeling happier than he had for a long time, with thoughts of his son playing in a garden.

Six months passed, during which time he served at different ports, and became proficient in the mechanics of the ship's engines, gradually rising up through the ranks.

The three friends were back at Portsmouth when they received orders to report for overseas duty. Much to their chagrin, they would be on different ships. But these were naval instructions and those serving in His Majesty's Royal Navy did not warrant a choice where they wished to be posted. To even think of challenging authority was tantamount to foundering a ship, and strong disciplinary action.

Shaking hands with one another, they hoped to meet up at one of the foreign British naval ports. Little did they realize their paths were never to cross again.

It wasn't long after mother and son moved into their new home, Violet found herself once again pregnant. Barely able to cope with moving into a house and looking after a fifteen-month-old boy, she wondered how she was going to manage without William who was somewhere sailing the high seas. Violet gave birth to her second son she christened Ralph.

William now held the rank of Petty Officer Engineer and was stationed at Malta when he received news of the birth of another son.

Whenever his ship docked at Singapore or Hong Kong, quicker than a wink, he hurriedly walked down the plank and headed to town looking for the best tailors where he ordered clothes to be made for his wife and children. Silk robes, satin lingerie, silk blouses, and handmade suits of the best quality material for his small sons. That he could enter any tailor's shop in these bustling cities early morning and return later in the day to pick up a new suit, left him pleasantly surprised.

'No wonder they prosper,' he said to himself.

One way he spent his hard earned money wisely was to buy tea and coffee sets of exquisite bone china in designs of bright red, gold and blue. A teacup when turned toward the light, showed the face of a geisha girl inside the bottom of the cup. The effect of the artist's work caused one to wonder how this image inside a cup could be effectively achieved, without cracking the delicate bone china.

William enjoyed these excursions, often alone, when his sea legs were on dry land. Browsing at leisure in the markets and stopping at various stalls, if he saw something he thought Violet would like he bought it without a second thought. When he presented her with gifts from the Orient, he studied her face as she opened each package and removed each item, with a curious eye. Perhaps wondering if there were other surprises, yet to unfold.

The oriental customs and cultures of Singapore and Hong Kong fascinated William. Keeping strictly within the rules of naval discipline when going in to town with other crew members, he avoided the pitfalls of accepting a friendly Chinese girl's invitation to show him a good time. Most invitations appeared innocent enough to sailors who had sailed the high seas for months, with only the crying birds or the creatures below the deep ocean for company, but to later discover they were tantalized with misguided thoughts, "fools suffer gladly", and end up with the pox. The excruciating pain on a sailor's face as he padded to the sick bay, was enough to steer William on the straight and narrow. He was determined not to be enticed to go down this avenue, and avoided it at all cost.

Hong Kong, formerly a desolate island, was occupied in 1841 by the British and became a colony. Its sole purpose was to create a trade centre free from Chinese control. In 1898 new territories of the Kowloon Peninsula and adjacent islands were added to the crown colony and leased to Britain for 99 years when the islands would be reclaimed by the Chinese.

Singapore became a separate crown colony in 1946. The city of Singapore is on the south shore. On the north shore is a British air and naval base area. When the country was invaded by the Japanese Malaya campaign in 1942, it was known as Shonan under Japanese occupation.

The Mediterranean island of Malta, another crown colony, was vital to the British defense line. During the Second World War, severe bombings damaged its art treasurers beyond repair. The Grand and the Marsamuscetto Harbours were fiercely guarded by the Allies to prevent serious damage to those Merchant Service ships carrying food and oil for the people of Malta, that needed to enter the harbour safely.

According to William, this was often a "miss and hit" run, as Malta was targeted relentlessly by the enemy to stop merchant ships from dropping off essential supplies to Malta. When the sirens wailed of an incoming attack, people fled to their concrete bunkers, fearful of what would greet them when they resurfaced to the sound of all clear.

San Francisco's Golden Gate boasts one of the finest harbours in the world. His Majesty's Royal Navy ships docked here on several occasions, with William aboard. When the locals, maidenly and matronly, heard or saw the ship was ready to dock, they welcomed the sailors with open arms.

He told me the story of one gentleman he and his Navy companions met, when they were downing a cool beer in one of the cocktail bars. He invited one and all back to his house. The party began in full swing and with justice to their host's hospitality, they sang and drank various wines and alcohol in the company of several beautiful Californian girls. He couldn't remember how the evening ended but it caused the entire Navy party to sleep well into the hours of next morning, thereby missing their ship as it sailed majestically out of San Francisco's harbour!

Of the many Navy tales I heard from my brother, this one, I thought, "takes the cake." I could but imagine the sheer look of surprise on their faces, knowing in the hours to come all would be required to face their captain with a full explanation.

Experiencing worldly travels, normally beyond his reach, William took to Navy life like a duck to water and revelled in a lifestyle second to none. His preference was the Pacific Ocean, rather than the cold Atlantic. His admiration of American hospitality overwhelmed him. He could not get enough of their free lifestyle and ventured to imagine perhaps one day he and his family would emigrate to the land of plenty. In his observation, the Americans did not differentiate in ranks. All members of the service were treated equally and royally.

The Second World War had been over for two years and the millions of people living across different continents were slowly getting their lives back to some normality. Britain continued to be under rations for food and other commodities until 1949. Many parts of Europe badly demolished of the essentials of life, looked toward the conquerors of the war to help them rebuild their lives and communities.

No longer wearing bell bottom trousers and his Navy blue hat slung on the back of his head, William now sported the uniform of Petty Officer, showing three gold strips on the sleeves of his jacket and wearing a white cap with a shiny black peak and the Royal Navy crest above. His official portrait taken in the studio of Kwong Ming, Hong Kong, shows the face of a happy man.

Back in the swing of ships, amid swirling oceans to foreign ports, he was acutely aware of his responsibilities not only to his King and country whose uniform he wore with pride for the second time, but to the family he left behind.

Two years prior to William's discharge from the Royal Navy in 1969, after completing 26 years service at the age of forty-five, my own family and I emigrated to Canada. Elizabeth and William kept in close touch with me, and we caught up with family news across both continents.

It was many years later when I learned of the numerous operations he had undergone during his time in the service. This turn of event came about on one of my visits to him, when he showed me the scars from the surgeon's knife that went round his entire body. I was horrified. It was like looking at a criss-cross section of railway lines that mapped the circumference of his inner organs, to remove one kidney. If other organs had been removed, he didn't say. Seeing the scars caused me to wonder if this was the reason why he endured so much pain, over the years.

While convalescing in one of the overseas hospitals, in order to keep his mind and fingers occupied, he learned the art of embroidery and rug-making, as an occupational therapy. The work he did was remarkable. I had to admit, I could not have done better, despite priding myself on being a first-class needle woman. What surprised me further, was to hear how he so thoroughly enjoyed doing embroidery or using a hook to make rugs, notwithstanding many of his cohorts who visited him in the hospital and teased him it was a woman's work. But he was not alone in this therapy, during a time of healing. Other patients in his ward took the same interest in a variety of artwork to keep themselves busy and created unusual designs and colours on canvas using either a brush or an embroidery needle, all looking quite professional.

Whenever I took it upon myself to question what his ship did at various British foreign ports he was reluctant to give full details, particularly if it was involved in some kind of political skirmish. Perhaps he thought he was still under the scrutiny of *The Official Secrets Act*. He never divulged information regardless of my being interested in it or not, perhaps with the view he had now left the service and to leave well enough alone.

The Island of Malta was a pivotal place of interest to most seamen, and the friendliness of its people was famous. The island's monkeys, however, kept everyone on the hop, locals and visitors alike who sat on the famous rocks eating food; this was a temptation for a monkey to grab the food from one's hand, without warning.

The population of Malta were dangerously close to starvation in the 1940s. By running the gauntlet through enemy air and land attacks, Allied Merchant ships were able to drop off supplies necessary for their survival. History records many Merchant ships and their crews were lost in supplying essential raw materials to other strategic points in and around the Atlantic regions. When William and I talked about this period in our lives, and surviving in different parts of the world, he would simply shake his head.

On one of our frequent ferry trips from Portsmouth to Shanklin, a sandy beach resort in the Isle of Wight, as soon as the ship docked, the family headed uphill to the only haberdashery shop in the small town to buy tablecloths, tea tray cloths, chair back covers and arm rests made from good linen. Also purchased were colourful skeins of Clarke's thread to use on the stencilled designs. This was one stop on my itinerary I did not want to miss. What surprised me though was the interest William took in every piece of linen I purchased. I had no idea then how talented he was with the sewing needle. It wasn't until we returned to his home

I realized his interest in embroidery work, as he studied the stencilled designs on each piece of linen. There was no stopping either of us after this. We chose to compete like soldiers on a battlefield, to see who could produce the best piece of needlework in design and colour. On par with my finger dexterity, William used the needle with remarkable skill.

Once our purchases were made in the haberdashery shop, we lunched at the local fish and chip restaurant, then made our way down to the sandy shore before catching the ferry back to Portsmouth. If the weather was good it made for an enjoyable day; however when it rained Shanklin was surely damp, cold and miserable.

PORTRAITS OF HIMSELF

Every other year I continued with my visits to the UK, and noticed Daniel and Ralph were getting close to six feet tall. Both were extremely good-looking. I wondered where this tallness in the family came from as their parents were of average height. Perhaps a throw-back to previous generations? Gentle Daniel had his mother's black curly hair. Ralph, who was the spitting image of his father, had yet to develop his sense of humour.

William was onboard ship out from the British Crown colony of Singapore, adjacent to Christmas Islands and Cocos Islands in the Indian Ocean, when Violet gave birth to her daughter Amanda, nearly ten years after the birth of her son Ralph.

In 1836 Charles Darwin based his coral-reef formation theory on observations made on Cocos Islands. These islands were discovered in 1609 by Captain William Keeling, hence the oft-used identification as Cocos (Keeling) Islands. They were first settled by Scottish and English merchants in the 1830s. The islands served as important air bases in Second World War.

The youngest child of the family, Amanda was horribly spoiled. She had only to sniffle, which caused her family to console her every need. Often, I watched William furtively slip a hand in his trouser pocket for a candy and pop it into her mouth when he thought no one was looking. I had no intention of interfering with the upbringing of his daughter, yet sensed somewhere down the road there would be consequences.

One Sunday morning William rang me with the news that ten-year-old Amanda had refused to go to school, because of her weight. Sensitive to innuendos from the other school children, she stubbornly cried, 'I don't want to go.'

Throughout our conversation I asked my brother if his daughter had been seen by their doctor. 'Perhaps he could refer her to a specialist,' I suggested, 'to help her emotionally and psychologically to deal with the problem.'

As though he had a ton weight on his shoulders, he grumbled. 'We've done that! Even took her to see a child psychologist. Nothing works.'

I felt sad to hear the stress in my brother's voice. Normally, a chirpy person who would prefer to laugh than cry, I sensed he was fraught to know which way to turn.

Trying my best to be helpful I made one or two suggestions, but imagined him holding the phone on the other end of the line, shaking his head.

After saying goodbye, I put the phone back on its cradle and sat on the edge of my bed trying to find an answer to my niece's weight problem.

You're certainly not alone having food concerns, I thought somewhat superciliously. Think of the world's starving children who would give anything to beg a crust of bread.

Although she was put on a strict low-carbohydrate diet and candy taboo, his daughter continued to put on weight.

On the advice of several doctor's recommendations, the local school board agreed to send a teacher and give Amanda her lessons at home. This arrangement with the school board worked well and although it helped the girl emotionally, it did not deal with the on-going weight problem.

Speaking with William on another occasion, I marvelled at his unusual philosophy. 'She'll grow out of it.'

'How?' I asked, totally unconvinced this philosophy would work.

William was right to have patience. Amanda, who could do no wrong and was the apple of her father's eye, continued with her studies at home and passed the exams which enabled her to go on to a commercial college in Havant. When she married an ex-Navy man, in the wedding photograph she did look slimmer. Years later, when I was visiting William and she came to see him, she was overweight but by then had given birth to three daughters.

William's ambition for his sons was to enrol them as apprentices in a trade that would provide them with a good future and sufficient income to support their own families.

Daniel began his apprenticeship as a carpenter. However, this trade was not to his liking and despite his father's encouragement to persevere, he decided to leave and seek employment in the car industry.

Ralph completed his apprenticeship to become a first-class motor mechanic, highly skilled in what is known in the UK as "car-bashing". Damaged cars repaired by him came off the loading bay, looking new. When speaking of his second son's achievement, William's face shone with pride.

The house in Cosham was eventually sold. Violet and William moved into a townhouse in Crookhorn, Hampshire where he spent much of his time in the garden and pottering around the greenhouse where he grew tomatoes and other plants, while continuing to hang on to every puff of a cigarette that never left his lips.

Crookhorn is a small town with few shops, but boasts one of the best pubs in the area, serving beer that tastes like beer. On a number of occasions when the family popped in for lunches or dinners William sat closest to the bar so he could chat up the barmaid, between eating

William, Caroline and Violet at the Rose and Crown, Hampshire.

and drinking. Violet sipped her drink, smiled, knowing he was enjoying himself, without compromise.

Everybody who is somebody in the neighbourhood, knows one another. Like most in his trade, the local baker was up before the crack of dawn preparing his dough in readiness for his regular customers. He sold freshly-made bread of all kinds. Crusty cobs on the top of which sat small rounds of breads, perfectly baked, known as cottage loaves. The best part of this loaf was to take the top layer off and smother it with butter. Hovis loaves, French sticks, Italian bread, buns and a variety of delicious small tarts. What caused me to drool at the mouth when inspecting his clean, wide shop windows displaying mouthwatering baked goods were the freshly made buns, some filled with cream, others with a pink glaze dribbled over them, enticing one's full attention to buy. The joy of taking a huge bite from one of the buns covered with pink glazed icing, was nothing short of pure ecstasy.

William at home in Crookhorn, Hampshire.

A daily ritual with the neighbours was to meet in the bake shop at an appointed hour. Chatting more than they purchased, this socializing often left the baker with a grim look on his face wondering if his hard work, rising so early each morning, would turn into much-wanted shillings and pennies to cover his supplies and costs.

Unbeknown to William, his baker friend was a keen photographer. One day, he asked if William would sit for him as he wanted to enter a competition for amateurs. William agreed, perhaps doubting his friend's talent as a photographer. They arranged to meet at a certain time after the bakery closed at the end of the day. Cautiously entering a small room at the back of the shop, William sat in the chair directed by his friend. With camera in hand the photographer clicked away, catching several poses of William in the eye of the lens including every line on his face, and mood of the moment. When he had finished the session, the baker thanked him, saying, 'See you.' My brother returned the friendly compliment,

William and Caroline in Crookhorn, Hampshire.

wandered off home, and didn't give the photographic session another thought.

Not long after he sat for his portrait, William entered the bakery shop to pick up supplies. Seeing a grin wide as a Cheshire cat on his friend's face, he asked, 'Big joke, or big win on the horses?'

'Lor! No, nothing like that.'

'What, then?'

'I won First Prize with your photographs.'

Thinking his friend was pulling his leg William laughed, 'You're having me on. I don't believe you. You're as bad or as good as me when it comes to jokes.'

Finally convinced what his friend said was true, William asked if he could see the photographs. He stood near the counter of the bake shop with the negatives in his hand, and studying them carefully, turned to his friend. 'Well, you certainly did a good job bringing out the wrinkles on my face.'

Customers standing inside the bake shop, with ears bent, listened to the two men who were doubled-up laughing, as though their heads would roll off. Curiosity got the better of one lady who inquired, 'What's to laugh about?'

The men were incapable of responding.

'Tell you what,' said William, finally getting control of himself as he put the negatives back in his friend's hand, 'when you close the shop, let's go to the local and celebrate your prize.'

After downing their last pint, the pair were in a state of euphoria over winning first prize, and having quenched their thirst, they left the pub shaking hands, and went home their separate way.

When my brother gave me a copy of his three portraits, all showed him in a pensive mood, cracking no humorous jokes. I wondered how the photographer managed to capture these images of him, knowing deep down he was aching for a laugh.

One portrait of him wearing a cap, shows a deep furrow between his brows. His mouth is firmly set. Studying the picture, I can't imagine it being my brother. He looks much too serious. In all probability, I reasoned, to compete in the competition there were standards of rules to follow, hence the studious expressions. The extraordinary interpretation of one portrait I have hanging on the living room wall is that wherever I sit, his eyes follow me. I like to think this is William's way of saying, 'I'm always with you.'

On a visit to William and Violet in the mid-1980s, Elizabeth and I took a day trip from London to Hampshire to spend time with them. The children had, so to speak, left the nest to get on with their own lives. We lunched at a pub in Crookhorn. As we sat enjoying a drink before lunch I was surprised to see Violet open her handbag and pull out a packet of cigarettes. Placing one between her lips, she waited for her husband to take his cigarette lighter to light it. Elizabeth and I looked at each other, perhaps with the same thought in mind. When did she begin to smoke?

Once seated on the train back to London I asked my sister, 'Did you know Violet smoked?'

She looked blank at me. 'No, this is the first time I've seen her with a cigarette.'

The subject dropped as we peered out of the train window, listening to the rhythm of the wheels as they skirted across Hampshire's beautiful countryside. Many woodland birds were seen in the fields. The chatterbox magpie with its black waistcoat and long tapering white tail, took precedent over all other feathered creatures, searching for food. Always on the ready to disappear when hawks or birds of prey appeared overhead, they could scatter among themselves in the trees.

With the continual rhythm of wheels speeding hard on the railway tracks, the train made its way from town to town and over the countryside of several villages. I looked at my sister who appeared in a dozing mood, and gave her a nudge. Glazed eyes questioned my action.

'Remember when we were children and we pinned sprigs of shamrock on our dresses to celebrate St. Patrick's day?'

'Mmmm,' came a sluggish response.

Trying to get a positive reaction from her, I nudged her again and pointed to the fields, as they flashed by. 'Don't they look as green as St. Patrick's shamrock?'

She nodded.

Life for William and Violet jogged along at a sleepy pace until the family visited with their children when it seemed all hell broke loose!

TURN OF EVENTS

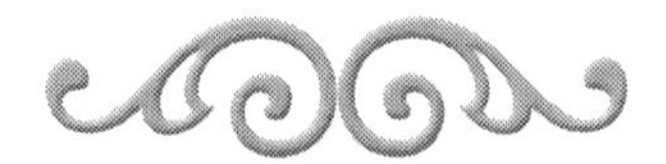

With his parents, Daniel and his sister Amanda came to Canada in 1974 to attend my daughter's wedding. After the marriage ceremony, the happy celebration began 2 p.m. at the Sherway Gardens in Islington, Ontario and continued on till 2 a.m. the following morning. Relatives from overseas who attended the wedding, were intent on having a good time in Canada. The house was not only filled to capacity with people but the swimming pool in the back yard seemed ready to burst at the seams as our visitors splashed about in it all hours of the night and day to cool off from the intense, humid heat.

I watched the activity with growing weariness and although I made a concerted effort to join in the fun I wondered which would flounder first, the swimmers or the drinkers. As the night of the wedding drew on I began to sway with exhaustion until finally I staggered to my bedroom, hopeful of a good night's sleep.

What should have been the normal run of things when organizing a wedding, turned out to be a round of bridal showers, tea parties, shopping for bridal and bridesmaids gowns, as well as ensuring the caterers arrived on time at the Gardens. Also, the large white ribbons hung upright on each wood knob down the side of the isles in the church.

Throughout their stay William and his family met friends of ours who were more than willing to entertain them until our guests from abroad left to fly back home, a few days after the wedding. It became obvious to everyone Daniel was showing a great deal of interest in our friend's eldest daughter.

Ontario's July weather, hot, humid and sticky, prompted us to leave the city of Mississauga and drive north of Toronto to cool off, somewhere in the country. Perhaps near a lake where a slight breeze off the water would be of benefit to everyone. This suggestion however did not appeal to my brother or his family. Instead, we drove into the city of Toronto and stopped for a buffet lunch at the restaurant on top of the then Eaton Centre.

Driving east of Toronto we headed to Black Creek Pioneering Village, off Jane Street, and visited several old farmhouses of bygone days. The smell of freshly-baked bread from the ovens, cooling on long wood trays, tempted one to buy a loaf. On another tray a portion of a loaf was cut into small pieces and lathered with fresh butter which we were invited to sample.

Entering the village schoolhouse, the smell of antiquity caused all noses to breathe in the musty air. The small wood chairs in front of miniature oak desks with inkwells, showed where the children had their lessons. A black stove near the front door had been the only source of heat for the schoolhouse. It appeared inadequate to provide sufficient warmth for the teacher and the students to concentrate on the lessons with cold hands and feet, during the bitterly cold winter months of Ontario.

Amanda began to drag her feet as we walked from one exhibit to the next, and moaned it was too hot. She wanted to sit down. William looked at me with concern and asked if their visit to the village could be cut short. Hyperventilating, I offered to drive his daughter back home to Mississauga while encouraging the rest of the family to stay, saying, 'It would be a shame not to see the village while you are here.'

When they returned home by coach it heartened me to hear, 'Wouldn't have missed it for the world.' That made my day!

The romance blossomed between the young couple across two

oceans and a year later, word came from Hampshire they were to become engaged. Daniel emigrated to Canada and quickly found work near Malton (now Pearson International) Airport. On a freezing cold winter day, with deep snow at the entrance of a small Presbyterian church in Streetsville, Ontario, the couple exchanged vows.

It was a simple ceremony with family and friends. Leaving the church to go to where the reception was being held, guests wearing long skirts tucked them up to avoid getting wet in the snow. My black patent shoes did not escape the heavy snowflakes.

The following year William and Violet visited them in their home in the small town of Streetsville, where the couple's first child was born. Three more children were to follow. Sadly, the marriage did not last.

A NEW RELATIONSHIP

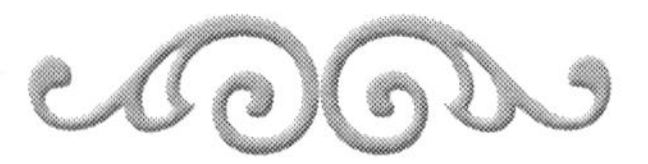

When our sister Elizabeth decided to emigrate to Canada in 1988, I was ecstatic! Not only would we see more of each other but also it would give me the opportunity to look after her fragile health. William, although pleased with the news to a certain extent, wished her well but didn't really want to see her go. He took her to dinner at the golf club two days before her departure on a nine-hour flight from Heathrow to Vancouver, then on to Victoria International.

When I met my sister at the airport she looked exhausted from the flight, peaked and thin. I suggested a few days rest to get her bearings, then we would go on ferry trips round the Gulf Islands, Salt Spring and Vancouver, taking in a buffet lunch on board, and enjoy the fresh air. I hoped it would give back her rosy cheeks.

After three years of living in one of the most beautiful places on Earth, her health much improved and gaining weight, Elizabeth shocked me with her decision to return to England. I was devastated beyond words – as though struck by a severe blow! Understanding her reason to leave was worse than trying to unravel a Chinese puzzle. It made no sense. 'Why,' I kept asking myself, 'does she want to go back to a life in the doldrums?'

As I struggled to find the missing pieces of reasoning why, I knew whatever triggered her decision to leave Canada was more than she was willing to divulge. She refused to go into detail and any comment I made, fell on deaf ears. She would not budge. I rang William with the news and asked if he would meet her at Heathrow when her flight arrived. Also, if he and Violet could accommodate her before she took off to the north of England, to fulfil her destiny to join a convent and be with God. This was her reason to leave Canada, I finally discovered. Sadly, her passionate desire to devote her final years with the Almighty did not pan out the way she anticipated. Her health worsened, which greatly concerned me. She returned to Hampshire several months later, a sad person.

I flew to England the following year and arrived at Heathrow. William, faithful as ever, waited for me at the arrivals. Generous to a fault, a taxi was ordered to take us to Crookhorn. Sitting hand-in-hand, in comparative silence, we looked out of the window as the car sped from one village to the next before it stopped outside his home. Elizabeth, all smiles, waving royally, was at the door to greet us. Looking at her appearance, loss of weight and pallor of complexion made me want to weep. 'Where in God's name is the justice in all this?' I thought.

Instead, I gave her a huge hug.

' Kettle's on,' she said, in worldly wisdom, giving me a weak smile.

When I was able to get William alone, he admitted she had been in and out of the hospital since leaving the north of England. Had God let her down? I convinced myself, it was not Elizabeth's fault her aspiring dream did not materialize. I felt vulnerable toward her.

'Why didn't you ring and tell me she wasn't well?' I whispered, feeling exasperated to the point of wanting to shout!

'I knew you'd worry, so decided not to,' he said in a quiet voice.

In the late eighties, Violet's health had deteriorated. On-going doctor's appointments did not show good results which meant William took care not only of their home, but also her everyday needs. When I visited them in 1989 I noticed she was much thinner than a year earlier. Her curved spine caused her head to drop on her chest. Sitting on a couch, it saddened me to see how ill she looked. What surprised me however, was how she managed to smoke a cigarette with her head down. I asked William if he thought it safe to leave her alone smoking, with a possible risk of catching her clothes on fire.

His brown eyes gave me a sad look. Trying to appear nonchalant, 'Well, I can't tell her not to smoke. It's whatever pleases her that matters,' he said in muted tones.

He may have sensed her life was coming to an end, and he did not have the courage to tell her to stop smoking.

Where William and Violet lived in the townhouse at Crookhorn, across the road from them was a small shopping arcade which included the bakery owned by his friend, the amateur photographer. One morning while they were out picking up supplies in the grocery shop, a loud bang from behind caused them to turn their heads. A well-groomed lady who looked in her early seventies, was bending down to retrieve fruit and vegetables that had fallen out of a large brown bag which had burst. For a second, William stood looking at the scene, then bent down to help the lady recover her goods. When they were put in a new bag, she thanked him. Peering into his brown eyes, 'I know you,' she said, 'you live across the street from me.'

When William and Violet introduced themselves to her, she told them her name was Marion and that she lived in the block of flats opposite where they lived. Rather than hold up their shopping time Marion said goodbye, with an invitation to drop by for a cup of tea. It wasn't until he and Marion met again at the arcade, he remembered their first meeting. She inquired about Violet's health and William told her his wife had not been well for some time.

'If you are in need of a break, why don't you pop in and see me,' she suggested.

He gave no more thought to the invitation until Violet ended up in the hospital at Cosham, where she was kept in for a few days. One morning, hearing a knock on his front door he wondered who this could be, as he was not expecting visitors. Upon opening the door, Marion was standing on the step holding a large bouquet of flowers.

'Sorry to burst in on you like this, but I heard your wife was taken to the hospital. These flowers are for her.'

William was dumbfounded. How did she know? He stood holding the door ajar and looked at Marion who was still standing on the doorstep, wondering if he would invite her in. Thanking her, he took the flowers from her, and asked if she had time to stop for tea.

Thereafter, on many occasions when I visited the family, if Violet was not up to it or was resting, I would either go with William or by myself to see Marion across the road. The first time I went to her flat it astonished me to see the luxury she afforded herself, but it wasn't until I knew more about her personal life did I realize how she was able to live, in stylish comfort. Her late husband had been an antique dealer. The home was crammed with antiquated vases, silver and chinaware, and carpeted in deep Indian and Persian rugs. The lifestyle she and her husband had lived was still maintained, and she kept pace with the upkeep and expense of running a beautiful home. Whenever we met, she looked and breathed affluence, exquisitely well-groomed, wearing expensive clothes, cosmetics, hairstyles and manicures,.

The relationship between William and Marion developed over the months, which came as a surprise. Despite being on opposite side of the social spectrum, the two seemed to hit it off. She was often seen by the neighbours darting in and out of his home, carrying fruit baskets and flowers. A year after my sister-in-law passed away in 1990, William saw more of his friend and often the two were seen in one of the local pubs having lunch, and downing a drink or two.

The memory I have of my sister-in-law Violet is her tremendous dry sense of humour. It would cause one to roll off a chair, if sitting in one, and laugh until ribs were ready to burst. Her face, dead-pan, showed not the slightest expression when making a joke. This side of her humour didn't really surface until her children were grown up, and left home. I remember an occasion when all the family grouped together in The Tudor Rose pub in the heart of Hampshire, to celebrate a birthday. A nook that seated eight, where a log fire burned brightly to give an atmosphere of warmth in a family environment, was booked ahead of time by William. Prior to ordering, he checked the menu to ensure it was to everyone's liking, particularly his wife's, who had a problem eating and digesting food. Drinks were offered before dinner.

Violet had been to her local hairdresser for the occasion, and looked well-groomed and chic in a lovely soft blue outfit and silk blouse. Chatting to his heart's content, William paused as the waiter approached our table and asked if we were ready to be served. The dinner placed before me looked appetizing to the point I wanted to start my meal before the rest of the family. At the same time, with an ear bent, I was anxious not to miss the conversation around me. Everyone was in a great mood to enjoy a nice family gathering. With a serrated edged knife, I gently inserted it in the breast of half a roasted chicken. To my surprise blood oozed from the breast and for a second, I sat poised with the knife in my hand and watched a trickle of blood fall on my plate. Seeing the look on my face one of my nephews asked if there was anything wrong. I held up the knife showing blood on the tip of it.

William saw the chicken was undercooked, and took centre stage. He beckoned to a waiter to come and remove my plate, and replace it with another meal. While I sat and waited for the waiter to reappear, the others began tucking in to their dinner.

Out of the blue, Violet chirped, 'It's neck wasn't wrung properly. That's why it's still bleeding.' Her face, expressionless.

Smiles appeared on everyone's face round the table, but no one spoke.

When the waiter placed the second plate in front of me I felt uneasy, seeing all eyes were upon me as though I were standing before a judge in a courtroom, awaiting his verdict. I picked up my knife and gingerly inserted it in the chicken breast. All was well. Drinks from glasses were

Weymouth Harbour.

once more sipped, and everyone relaxed. The chicken was tender and fully cooked. However, Violet once more chirped, 'Chickens are a bit stupid to be caught and eaten,' as she opened her mouth to put in a slice of breast.

'Well,' said her youngest son, 'the sole purpose of breeding them is for food, isn't it?'

Violet, no longer interested in discussing the breeding of chickens, simply went on eating.

The relationship between my brother and Marion appeared purely platonic until his wife passed away, when it developed into something more meaningful. The two met frequently, and enjoyed

William with friends at Weymouth, 1998.

excursions by ferry to the Isle of Wight and other islands close to the French border. William started taking more trips to Weymouth when he discovered her daughter lived there. It was in the plans for mother and daughter to share a house once Marion decided to leave Crookhorn and move to Weymouth.

Due to an age gap between the couple, I took it for granted the relationship was going nowhere. That is, until not long after Violet's death, I was stunned to learn he had made a proposal of marriage to Marion. Months went by, and as they surged ahead with wedding plans, the two were seen in town like a pair of cooing doves. All appeared to be going well when, out of the blue, he telephoned and told her he had second thoughts and the wedding was off. Marion's daughter, Janet, was quick to step in after seeing her mother so distraught with the news. At a flick of an eyelash, she went to see William and tried to make him see reason then told him, in no uncertain terms, he would be sued for breach of promise.

Living in Western Canada, it was too far for me to get involved in the unfolding drama. At the time I asked myself why my brother, who had always been a fair judge of character of the people he met, why he faulted on this occasion. Perhaps it was a case of being caught on the rebound, after the death of his wife.

To avoid a court case, the couple arrived at an amicable settlement. Despite the agreement being reached, Janet insisted her mother be reimbursed for her new bridal outfit, plus all expenses paid by her for the wedding reception. Forever consciously careful with his income, William found he was forced to pay up a few thousand pounds. Months later when speaking with me over the phone, I sensed he was of the opinion it was a stroke of luck he wasn't taken to the cleaners for breach of promise. He could have lost his shirt!

Fate has a way of leading us along the paths of fortune or misfortune, often taking us completely by surprise. A year after the settlement for dissolution of the marriage, William was spending a week alone at Weymouth, during the month of July. Relaxing in a leather chair outside a cafe, watching the world go by, and enjoying a cup of coffee, a tap on his shoulder caused him to turn his head. Standing above him was a smiling Marion, perfectly groomed. Taking the chair beside him, she sat down. This encounter should not have come as a total surprise because he knew Marion had now moved from Crookhorn and was sharing a house with her daughter, near Weymouth harbour. Never one to hold a grudge he was of the opinion what happened in the past, is history, and offered her a cup of coffee.

They sat chatting for a while and when she was about to leave, asked William how much longer he would be staying at Weymouth. He told her two days. 'With luck, we might run into each other again before you go back to Crookhorn,' she said.

Giving her a grin, he left the cafe and walked in the direction of the Crown Hotel where he was staying.

A few days after he returned home, fate once more played its hand. The telephone rang in his living room and picking up the receiver, he heard Marion's voice on the other end of the line. This came as no surprise to him.

'Thought I'd ring, after our chance meeting at Weymouth,' she said, in breathless tones.

William sat in a chair listening, as she chatted on. It wasn't until she told him she would be in Crookhorn for a few days visiting a friend, did his ears perk up.

'For old-time sake, can we go for a drink somewhere?'

The two arranged to meet at a favourite pub in town. As one drink led to another, the tension between them became more relaxed. Marion told him about the house where she and her daughter lived near the harbour at Weymouth, and said she was happy living there. Although it was on the tip of her tongue to extend an invitation to him, she knew he would refuse because her daughter Janet had accused him in the past of being irresponsible.

To all intent and purpose, the romantic flame had not burnt out completely. The months following the visit to Marion's friend in Crookhorn, led to more frequent ones. By this time her daughter was becoming suspicious why her mother was spending more time in Crookhorn, and was convinced the visits to her friend were not entirely the real reason. William also sensed Janet knew he had renewed his friendship with her mother but what she was unaware of, they were spending week-ends together.

They enjoyed the Isle of Wight; it being within easy reach and a shorter ferry ride from Portsmouth, than going to the Channel Islands. The week's forecast for warm and sunny weather seemed a perfect time for them to sit and enjoy the sunshine from their hotel room, overlooking the harbour, and watch the ferries come and go. With some trepidation, William suggested to Marion she tell her daughter of their plans to spend a few days in the Isle of Wight, prior to their leaving Portsmouth. This did not happen.

The hotel where they stayed was their haven. The first day or two all went well. They spent time on the sandy beach, and stopped to chat with the local fishermen by the harbour after they had drawn in their nets, loaded with fish. Linking arms, the couple went in search of places of interest.

Being a small island, there was little to choose from the small shops; however, with an eye for detail in good pieces of antiques Marion encouraged William to go with her to the one and only place where they were bought and sold. Deliberating over the price of a porcelain figurine with the owner, Marion told him she was interested but not prepared to pay the amount he was asking. As the two bartered and finally came to an agreement on the price, William stood by without saying a word. He wondered where she would find room in her house to put another piece of antique.

Friday being their last night at the hotel William wanted to make it special by inviting Marion to her choice of restaurant, where they could relax over dinner. After leaving the restaurant they decided to take a walk and stretch their legs before having a final nightcap, and retire to bed. At the hotel bar William ordered two glasses of whiskey, which he took back to their room. Sitting in easy chairs side by side, the couple heartily agreed it had been a good week not only with their accommodation but also the weather, for once, remained bright and sunny.

Marion suddenly stopped talking in mid-sentence, and placed a hand on her chest. William looked at her and asked if she was all right. She responded by patting her chest, and gave him a weak smile. 'It's probably indigestion, and nothing to worry about.'

He took the glass from her hand and put it alongside his on the table in front of them. Putting his arms round her shoulders, she appeared to relax. He then walked her to the side of the bed. When her breathing became more distressed, he gently held her in his arms, not wishing to leave her alone to run to the reception desk to ask for a doctor. Then, without warning, she collapsed and died in his arms. It was a massive stroke. William placed Marion gently on the bed. Reaching for the telephone on the night table he rang the receptionist at the front desk, and briefly explained what had happened. He asked if she would telephone for the police.

When the police arrived to question him about his identity, and asked Marion's name, he felt embarrassed when they recorded two different surnames. He asked himself why he did not have the courage, second time round, to ask her to marry him. Not only losing the dear friend she had become, he now had the task of facing her daughter about the events that took place, and this concerned him. Marion admitted to him when they arrived at the hotel that she did not tell Janet of their plans to spend a week together because she felt her daughter might spoil it.

Some things in life are stranger than fiction. Despite the hostility between Janet and William when he called off the wedding, it did not leave a sour taste in either one's mouth. Years later, Janet realized my brother did love her mother and had the greatest respect for her, despite their age gap, and that eventually they would have married.

Three years after Violet's death in 1990, William and I visited Elizabeth who was now in a nursing home at Horndean, Hampshire. She was well taken care of by the staff, whose sole interest was the welfare of the residents. Sitting in a soft armchair, William to one side of her, me on the other side, trying not to sound too emotional, I talked about her life in Canada and how happy she had been with her newly-found friends, and her church. Although desperately wishing she could come back to Canada with me, I realized I was clutching at straws, in the hope she had the strength to make the journey across an ocean and a continent. Instead, I gave her a goodbye hug. Reaching for the door, I turned back to look at her. She gave a weak smile and a wave. A lump came up in my throat. Trying to hold back the tears, I returned her smile. Quietly closing her bedroom door, we left.

Leaving the nursing home William and I linked arms, lost in thought, and worried if she would survive another year.

Not long after my return to Canada, William received a phone call from the nursing home to say Elizabeth had had a relapse. He rang me with the news and said he would stay with her to the end.

Hearing my sister had passed away, despite knowing her health had hung on a fine balance, I was devastated. This was a sister whom I adored and in essence, everything I wanted to be. Despite having different train of thoughts on controversial subjects in world affairs, our family ties remained entwined.

THE CHUNNEL

In August 1994, with my sixteen-year-old granddaughter Christine, I travelled from Vancouver to London, England, and arrived at Heathrow 11:30 a.m. the following morning. William and his taxi driver were waiting for us at arrivals. On our way to Hampshire I pointed out to Christine the names of the small villages we passed, in the hope a first visit to England would remain a happy memory. Once we had recovered from jet-lag, I was anxious to show her as much as possible the country where her grandparents were borne and bred.

A week after our arrival at William's home, we took the bus mid-morning from Crookhorn to Portsmouth, where we lunched and shopped. Time spent looking at clothes in a variety of stores became lots of fun, as Christine skipped through racks of dresses, shorts and blouses. Encouraging her to have whatever fits and pleased her, we laughed so much on these shopping expeditions, our ribs hurt.

As William had generously paid for my granddaughter's air fare, I asked if he minded us taking a few days to visit Paris. I had visited Paris in 1950, when I stayed at Étretat, a resort on the Normandy beach, then had another visit, in 1952. Paris is a city not only of great history, but also bursting with vitality. Its theatres of opera and ballet are second to none. William whole-heartedly agreed his great-niece should see as much as

Caroline in Paris, 1994.

possible of England and France, to give her a wider perspective how people lived in other countries.

In Portsmouth we stopped at the offices of Thomas Cook, where I bought tickets from London to Paris, via the Chunnel. Before leaving Hampshire, William gave me the telephone number of a friend living in Paris. ‹Just in case you need help. One never knows what might turn up in a foreign country.› His foresight saved us many anxious moments.

Taking the bus to Havant, we boarded the train to London and from there, picked up the express to Paris. Going through the Chunnel did not take as long as I expected. It was less than thirty minutes. The express pulled in to Gare Saint-Lazare. Amid the hustle and bustle of travellers, we edged our way to the Metro for Saint-Denis.

We arrived at our hotel on the east side of the city. When shown to our room it did not please me, neither did the location. A request to the proprietor to be put in a room of better standing, was agreed. The next morning I rang William's friend, explaining our predicament. Hearing a slight gasp on the phone, I expressed my intent to get Christine and me away from what I deemed an undesirable area, and undesirables lurking out of hotel windows. Without hesitating, she agreed to book us in a hotel near the Eiffel Tower.

'Just mention my name. All will be taken care of to make you comfortable. Ring if you need more help,' she bubbled in a clear English voice.

A taxi took us across the city of Paris. I was so delighted when we arrived at the hotel, I offered a handful of franc notes to our driver, who spoke no English. Our room was splendid with a balcony view of the Eiffel Tower, and a panoramic scene of the city. The bathroom held a deep luxurious bath, to wallow in.

We had visits to the Eiffel Tower, where activities continued well into the early hours of the morning. A trip to the Louvre surprised Christine when she saw the portrait of the Mona Lisa in a small frame, for so great an art treasure. Rodin's sculptor of The Thinker caused us to stop and stare.

We left Paris at Saint-Lazare station to catch our scheduled journey on the express, via the Chunnel. As we entered the station we noticed many gendarmes were gathered outside, apparently having been warned of a possible terrorist attack. We hurried to where the train was stationary and boarded, back to London.

When we arrived at William's home, I knew he was eager to hear our news. I mentioned our experience in the hotel booked by Thomas Cook.

'Good thing I gave you my friend's phone number in Paris,' he remarked. 'Told you, one never knows.'

Christine and I returned to the offices of Thomas Cook. Asking to see the manager, a well-groomed lady, she took us to her office. Without further ado, I placed all expenses I had incurred on the trip on her desk, plus tips to the taxi driver who took us across Paris. I politely suggested to her, I wished to be fully reimbursed. Checking all the receipts, the manager assured me all expenses would be paid in full. As we left her office, I looked at Christine's expression, one of disbelief. I said, 'It is a lesson learned. But in the analysis, how you present a problem is what gives one the satisfaction of achieving a goal, without confrontation.'

LONGSTANDING FRIENDSHIP

In September 1995, I was back in England to stay with William in Hampshire. Before leaving Canada I phoned to say I would like to spend the first week in England with a dear friend who lives in Orpington, Kent. He was comfortable with my plans and, with his on-going generosity, said he would arrange for his usual taxi driver to pick me up at Heathrow Airport and drive me to Orpington, then return and take me to Hampshire. All went smoothly with these arrangements, and I was extremely grateful to my brother who cared for my safety in getting me from one county to the other. Our driver, smiling, was waiting at arrivals, and picked up my luggage.

We drove out of the maze of traffic at Heathrow Airport and headed through countryside in the surrounding areas of Kent that was reminiscent of the many walks I took, when a child. My eyes scanned the green fields hoping there was a remote chance of catching a glimpse of caravans of the Romney gypsies who in the 1920s and '30s lived off the land, but there were none.

When the driver pulled up outside my friend's house I offered a gratuity, which he politely refused, saying, 'Your brother has taken care of it.'

My friend Audrey and I have been long-standing friends going back to the 1960s, when our husbands met for the first time in a pub at Tolworth, Surrey and thereafter became frequent drinking buddies.

Sunday teas at my friend's house were equal to William's dinner of roast beef and Yorkshire puddings. Salad plates were piled high with a variety of greens, ham, eggs and beets with cherry tomatoes piled on top, a position which often caused them to fall off the plate and roll to the floor. Huge slices of Angel cake, bought from Mark and Spencers, topped Sunday teas.

Prior to moving to Orpington, Audrey and her second husband, having divorced her first husband, some years later moved to Biggin Hill, Kent, where they ran a beer and wine bar at the airport.

Biggin Hill is nationally known for its airfield, where famous fighter squadrons played an outstanding part in the Battle of Britain and the air warfare which followed. Mementoes of its "finest hour" are provided by the Hurricane and Spitfire which flank the main gates and by the Memorial Chapel with its twelve stained-glass windows commemorating the squadrons stationed here.

My memories go back to childhood days during the Second World War, when I watched dog-fights over the airport and picked up pieces of shrapnel after a raid. Kent was heavily bombed in the strategic areas near the white cliffs of Dover. It was an important naval base and chief port for Dunkirk evacuation, and was under constant fire from Germany's long-range guns in France. Subterranean caves and tunnels in the cliffs served as shelters.

A regular visitor to the airport was a red tail fox who calmly ignored all activities on the airstrip and in the early hours of the morning, ambled to the outside of the bar where my friend left his breakfast in a bowl. As though on a timed schedule, he disappeared in the nearby bushes when the pilots headed to the bar for breakfast of bacon and eggs, where my friend was happy to cook and feed hungry men.

Audrey's black cat named Barney terrified most living creatures who risked life and limb when daring to approach the airstrip or the bar. Watching the fox closely with his green eyes, Barney knew the time and place when this invited visitor arrived, and never lost sight of his tail. Having satisfied his stomach, the fox ambled back to his den. One particular morning, several pilots were chatting near the airstrip and stopped speaking when they spotted the fox with an apple in its mouth, as it sauntered alongside the strip, without fear, and disappeared in the bushes. They all set off to the bar, laughing their heads off!

Barney's early morning routine was to sit outside the entrance to the bar with his front paws firmly clasped together and his sharp green eyes on the alert for four-legged intruders. Often he sat watching the young pilots joking among themselves, as they casually strolled to the bar to eat a hearty breakfast. Most of them he knew by sight and when they stopped to stroke his back, it caused Barney to purr softly. He liked that!

On the other hand, his green eyes remained focused on any intruder who dared to invade his territory. As though on a timed brain signal for action to attack, his sharp claws were on the ready to pounce. For the enemy, there was no escape.

One of the pilots once asked me who would win between the two in a confrontation. My response was that although Barney has sharp claws and a wit about him, the red tail would probably win being more cunning of the two.

ANOTHER MOVE

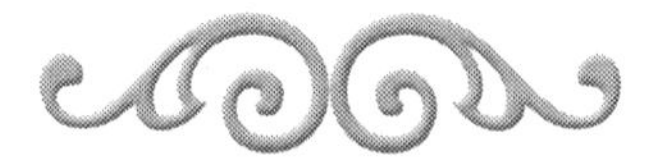

After the sale of the Crookhorn property, William moved into an apartment at Waterlooville, a larger town, not far from where he previously lived. Waterlooville is a town in Hampshire, England, approximately 8 miles north of Portsmouth. It has a population of about 20,000 and is surrounded round Purbeck, Cowplain, Crookhorn, Denmead, Horndean and Widley. It forms part of the South Hampshire conurbation. The town formed around the old A3 Portsmouth Road. The southern boundary is the coastline of the English Channel and the Solent, facing the Isle of Wight.

William's gregarious nature, so aptly developed during his days in the Navy, had not changed since Violet's death, although I sensed a slightly less rapport to his new neighbours with whom he wanted to give a wide berth, perhaps thinking he was not ready or willing to take a second wife. Living alone, as part of the human process, he was of the opinion life could only get better, not worse. It caused him to rethink the importance of each waking day, and dwell on the many hours he spent in the garden and greenhouse at Crookhorn, which he now missed. To divert from the regular routine and environment of living in an apartment, he frequently went by taxi into Portsmouth where he stopped off for lunch at one of the local pubs, and commiserated with any serving sailors whom he happened to meet.

Amanda and her three children lived close by, and frequently visited. As with his own daughter, spoiling his granddaughters came easy, as he cuddled and petted each child on his knee, one hand surreptitiously dipped in his inside trouser pocket to pull out a favourite candy and pop in the child's mouth, hoping Mother wasn't looking.

Here we go again. On each of my visits when the children came to see their grandfather, my brother knew I was watching, and gave me a "don't-tell" grin.

Although sorely tempted to suggest, 'How about a nice piece of carrot?' I held my tongue.

Second son Ralph often called in to see his father after work. He is an intelligent young man with whom I had much in common until one day, we had an irreconcilable difference.

Over the years, apart from Daniel, there was a certain amount of resentment from the rest of William's family whenever I visited. However, Ralph did not show the same attitude or jealous nature toward me as his sister, who caused me to shy away from her. Since their mother's death, rumbles of discord were heard in the distance when we went on our yearly visit to the Crown or the King's Head at Weymouth, but neither William nor I allowed it to spoil our days together. These were great times when we strolled at leisure along the sandy beach, breathing in the salty ozone from the ocean, laughing, and tuned in to the life around us.

The Crown seldom lacked tourists but if one didn't book accommodation ahead of time there was the possibility of not being able to get a room. Coaches from all parts of England came to the Dorset coast, for its balmy sea air, and sandy beaches. Seniors' tours from the northern part of the country frequented this coastline during the summer months, also at Christmas.

Life at Waterlooville continued apace. Gradually settling down in his apartment, on a cold day, William sometimes took afternoon tea with the ladies in the residence lounge where they sat in armchairs sipping hot tea, made in the kitchen nearby. When he "graced" them with his company he often brought with him one of his sponge cakes. This delighted the ladies who were eager to sample a slice, while exchanging local gossip. Occasionally, the group arranged to split the cost of meals brought in from the fish and chip shop or a pub, which saved them from having to cook the evening dinner.

On the lower floor in the apartment block a well-furnished room, with bathroom and shower, was available to the owners to rent for family members and friends. I stayed at this small suite on a number of occasions and found it comfortable and clean. The place was so quiet, one expected to be able to get a peaceful night's sleep. But hearing the sound of a barking fox kept me awake at all hours until whatever tricks he was up to, the noise finally abated and I was able to nod off into no-man's land.

On many of my visits I brought with me a variety of garments, if William hinted on the phone he was soon to run out. I had visions of him throwing the old ones out and using the new ones I bought him. Not so! At one point, I decided to help him clean and tidy his linen cupboard and much to my surprise found newly-packaged Canadian garments still in their plastic covers, left unopened.

'William,' I said, 'thought you were low on these items, so how is it you haven't used them.'

He gave me the proverbial grin that caused me to grin and say, 'Well, I guess when you're ready to throw out the old ones, you will wear them?'

Time proved otherwise. We grew up with the philosophy never to waste, or throw anything out, until it disintegrated. It was an English trait going back to the days of rationing during the war when every man, woman and child, learned to make-do-and-mend. Conserve and preserve.

William would pop into the local bookies in town, not only to place bets, but spend time with other gamblers who enjoyed smoking and exchanging local and family gossip. Having joined him at the bookies on many occasions I found his group of friends eager to give me tips on a favourite, to win. At first, I shied away from this line of entertainment but found myself caught up with the enthusiasm of the players as they puffed on cigarettes and loudly cheered a winner, racing across the wide screen on a wall. Small bets placed by me, on the advice of one of them, often resulted in a winner. When I told William I had won, he remarked, 'Beginner's luck.'

The Thursday markets held in Waterlooville often left me wondering where all the vendors came from with their variety of merchandise that was priced higher, on some items, than one could buy in the local shops. My brother was not interested in joining me on these excursions he found boring. Although I wasn't exactly enthralled with the saleable goods, I ventured to trot from stall to stall in the hope something of interest would catch my eye, sufficiently enough for me to buy. When I returned home empty-handed, William didn't comment.

I said, 'Usual stuff, not even a plant to bring home.'

A CASE OF SHINGLES

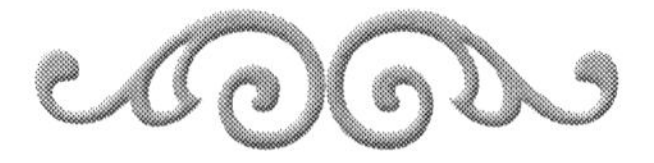

In May 1996, with my eldest brother Rowland, who had emigrated to Canada three years earlier, I boarded an overnight flight from Vancouver to Heathrow where our first cousin whose name was also Elizabeth, arranged to meet us at the airport. Our cousin owned a large house in its own grounds, sharing it with her daughter and son-in-law. Both were delightful people, and very welcoming.

Part of the land at the back of the property was left in its natural state, uncultivated, while the surrounding areas were professionally landscaped with trees, shrubs, and flowering perennials covered in blossoms. In the centre of the garden an arbor made of trelliswork held clematis and other climbing plants. On the south side, all kind of vegetables and as many different fruit berries were grown. The wide stone-laid terraces leading from the front of the house cascaded with aubrietia and other rock plants including snowdrops and crocuses. Tall black wrought-iron gates opened at the press of a button on a wall, to allow visitors to enter.

A small hotel nearby was booked ahead and upon arrival from the airport, we were shown into comfortable rooms. Our plans were to spend a week in Sussex and revisit Tunbridge Wells, a favourite and historical borough 15 miles SW of Maidstone, Kent. A "Royal Borough," it was once a fashionable spa. Chalybeate springs were discovered here in

1606. Noted visitors included Queen Anne, Dr. Johnson, Garrick and Thackeray, literary writers and poets. A promenade, called Pantiles, is lined by a colonnade and lime trees. Nearby are curious sandstone formations. "Tunbridge" wooden mosaics were noted. Having spent a leisurely day touring the borough and picking up one or two pieces of china at one of the many antique shops, and taking advantage of the warm weather to sit and enjoy the garden, our visit over, Elizabeth offered to take us by car to Crookhorn where I was anxious to see William living alone after Violet's death in 1990. (Three years later we were to lose our sister Elizabeth.)

On this particular visit, thinking of the two people who held a special place in my heart, I stopped to reflect on happier days when Violet's dead-pan face never creased a smile while she told jokes, and caused those around her to laugh until sides ached. I am sure this trait stemmed from William throughout their marriage because when I first met Violet she gave the impression of being quietly reserved and seemingly unknown for this kind of humour.

Our sister Elizabeth was well-read, and had a love of meeting people in all walks of life from monks to baronesses, cardinals and canons, a Spanish count. She remained to the rest of her life unaffected by those who passed through her life, and took it as a gift from God in whose faith she never faltered.

After spending a week with cousin Elizabeth, she drove us to see William. Because he had come down with a severe case of shingles we thought it best we did not stay with him. When we arrived at Crookhorn, he was standing outside his front door to welcome us. His face was red and blotched and not being able to hug him or go in the house for a cup of tea, saddened me, as we stood near the gate talking like strangers. For the rest of our visit in the UK we stayed at Southsea. Even the sunshine failed to put a smile on my face as my thoughts were with William whose hugs and jokes spun golden rings of pleasurable years together at Dorset.

Daily, in Southsea, I rang to ask how he was, and told him how we spent our days, mainly sitting on a long stone wall facing out to sea that

Southsea Castle.

stretched for miles above the shoreline of a beach of pebbles. Ferries leaving from Southsea harbour went back and forth in slow motion. As we sat silent each with our own thoughts, to a degree, this visit was enjoyable although something was missing and I knew only too well what it was – William. Of all the years we spent precious time together, it would take a severe case of shingles to disrupt what we termed, "our time together."

A SECOND WIFE

The year 2001, William decided to spend Christmas at the Crown. 'To get away from the hustle and bustle of Hampshire,' as he put it.

It was here he met a vivacious lady named Darlene, who was with a coach party from the northern part of the country. She was a widow with grown-up children. The regular evening's entertainment of bingo, dancing and drinking is how the two met, in the hotel bar. Never one to be known short of coming forward, William asked if she would like to go to Portland Bill and lunch with him. Giving him a questioning look she laughed, thinking it a joke, 'are you serious?'

Stubbing out a lighted cigarette, he peered into eyes brown as his own. 'Wouldn't ask if I wasn't serious, would I?'

At the end of the holiday, Darlene left Weymouth to return home to Nottingham and promised to keep in touch. Over the following months they rang each other daily, and on birthdays exchanged gifts. Often, on the spur of the moment, William would send her flowers.

I arrived back the following Spring at Heathrow airport, where William and his taxi driver were waiting to greet me. Once my suitcase was put in the trunk, and we were seated in the back of the car, William slipped his arm through mine as though to say 'life's great!,' when out of the blue he blurted, 'I'm thinking of getting married.' I almost fell out of my seat!

'Good God, you can't be serious,' I whispered, hoping the driver wasn't listening to our conversation.

He simply grinned, 'Well, you'll meet her soon.'

'I can hardly wait,' I said.

Catching my breath, I spluttered, 'When, and where did you two meet?'

At the back of my mind I immediately thought this is one of his lady friends he meets often at Asda. Then I remembered most of them were already married and their spouses thought William was forever blasting off like cannons in mid-ocean, when he chatted them up.

'What's her name?' I said in whispered tones.

'Darlene.'

'You're not really serious, are you?' I questioned.

'Wait until we get home, I'll give you all the news over a cuppa.'

Patience stirs the mind in thinking, I hope it's worth the wait.

Once we arrived home and settled comfortably in soft chairs, cups of tea in our hands and munching on Peak Frean biscuits, I was agog for news. William however was more intent on giving me the full story of his romance only after the tea cups had been washed and dried, and put back in the kitchen cupboard. With a wide grin on his face, he told me he had decided to spend last Christmas at the Crown Hotel at Weymouth where in the entertainment and bar room, bingo is played nightly. This is where the two lovers met.

Widowed early in life, Darlene is the mother of three children. One lives close by her in Nottingham; two other daughters live in the south of England.

Although a strong relationship developed over the months between the two, fate deemed it would not survive. The distance between north and south of England presented a difficulty of mileage from the beginning of the romance. The adage, absence makes the heart grow fonder, works for some lovers, but in William's and Darlene's case their early romance was conducted through telephone wires, rather than in person, and did not give them the opportunity of seeing the expression of love on their faces as it would, had they lived in neighbouring towns.

Darlene, with her bubbly and carefree nature, struck me as being the perfect second wife for my brother. However, when his younger son and daughter became aware of their father's relationship with a widow living in the north of England, she was shunned every step of the way.

With an emphatic, 'No, definitely no, we don't want her as a step-mother,' their voices pounded in William's ears.

On one trip when Darlene went to Hampshire, the lovers only recourse was to secretly meet in one of her daughters' home at Farnham. This, of course, was not the normal run of a love affair whereby a loving couple had to steal whatever time they could to be with one another by meeting at a secret rendezvous, to avoid confrontation by family members. Prior to leaving home, Darlene telephoned William so he could book a hotel room in advance of her arrival, and be within easy reach of where she was staying. It gave him an opportunity to meet Darlene's daughters, who later turned out supportive of him as a future step-father.

In September of the same year, I was back again at Heathrow Airport and our usual driver was the only one to greet me. William had warned me ahead of time, without revealing the reason, he would not come to the airport. We stepped outside to the waiting taxi, in brilliant sunshine. There was not a cloud in the sky. I hoped the warm weather would continue throughout my stay and that the heavy clothing I had brought with me, would not be needed. But as is the norm with the English climate, warm can turn to cold within seconds, so on each visit I was prepared to face the elements with raincoat and umbrella.

Once seated, we left the busy terminal and were on our way from London to Waterlooville, travelling through small country villages and farmers' fields of lush green. Magpies, with their long tapering tails and black and white plumage, strutted noisily among other smaller birds, fighting for the best feed. In meadows of gold, cows pastured, and skylarks flew singing high into the air. Hawks were seen flying over a field on the look-out for any hare, rabbit, mice or mole that slipped out of its nest at an inopportune time.

We were halfway across Hampshire when the driver stopped at a service junction. I was puzzled. Normally, he never pulled up for gas on any of these trips and it was not until I saw two heads pop out from under the bushes did I realize what was happening. I had barely stepped out of the car when William grabbed my arm. Amid much laughing and hugs he introduced me to my future sister-in-law, a bubbly personality. The driver, who was part of this charade, watched the performance with a wide smile on his face. His three passengers, giggling like school children, scrambled in the back seat of the taxi, as our driver took the wheel and headed across country roads. For once, I was too busy trying to catch up with the news to look at the beautiful scenery of Hampshire, as it flashed by.

When we reached the warmth of William's apartment, although I was dying to put my head down for a nap after a long flight, I tried to stay alert. I wanted to know everything about how the two met. Was it love at first sight? After cups of tea, and listening to the laughing going on round me, I headed to the bedroom where I collapsed on soft blankets.

On this particular visit, throughout my stay, I listened to the chatter of two happy people sitting close together on the couch in the living room, oblivious to my presence. Bong, bong, bong, tripped the big hand of the old clock above the mantlepiece as it touched the appointed hour, and caused them to look in my direction. The two arose off the couch. William suggested taking a taxi to Waterlooville, where we stopped at a pub and had a leisurely lunch. After what I considered an appreciable number of drinks I sat quietly listening about their future plans, with one ear. The other ear was cocked in the direction of pub drinkers who were laughing and spluttering in their beer mugs, as they clung to the bar counter.

Most days, I left the two alone to enjoy time together, and took the bus to Portsmouth which left from a bus stop on the main road nearby.

A week or two after arriving back in Canada, my brother rang to give me the exciting news he had proposed to Darlene and she was coming back to Hampshire. I offered my congratulations but declined the invitation to their engagement party, due to commitments at home.

When news of this happy event reached his daughter and younger son they exploded, and did their best to convince him the only reason this lady was interested in him, was for his money. I could barely contain my composure when hearing the news and wondered how William could be denied finding happiness the second time round, when he had always been an excellent father to them. It was a great disappointment to him his family refused to attend his engagement party. Neither were they willing to recognize, nor would they accept Darlene as their future step-mother.

I arrived back at Heathrow Airport mid-July 2003, where William was waiting to greet me with our taxi driver. He showed us where he had parked his car in the drafty terminal and picking up my suitcase, placed it in the trunk. Once seated in the back of the vehicle, William slipped his arm through mine and began chatting about his wedding and where the marriage ceremony and reception were to be held. Both agreed on a small wedding, with family members and a few friends of Darlene's from Nottingham.

As always the case in Portsmouth, sailors took advantage of time away from shore base to lap up a pint or two at the bars, while keeping a close eye on those coming through the swing doors of the pub. Noted for providing not only good hot meals of fresh vegetables, pub's prices were far more reasonable than lunches bought in cafes or in the one department store at Portsmouth.

Saturday morning in Portsmouth intrigued me with its hustle and bustle of fruit and meat vendors, chanting their wares to entice housewives of the best prices. I often went alone to the market and found it more interesting because it was run by the locals rather than a conglomerate of foreigners who rented the stalls at Waterlooville and charged outrageous prices for poor quality merchandise. I came home one day from the Portsmouth market with a small bag of potatoes grown in Egypt, much to William's surprise. And a pair of new running shoes.

Darlene was back in Hampshire, a week after my arrival, and stayed at a local hotel with her friends from Nottingham. The days prior to the wedding were much like those of any other couple getting married. We shopped together at Portsmouth for my outfit and after traipsing from one store to the next, I finally chose one that had colours of red, beige and cream. Amid the thronging crowds and shopping at Portsmouth for my outfit, Darlene and I came back to the apartment exhausted.

The night before the wedding William and I sat chatting in the living room. He appeared in a state of nervousness so I asked, 'What's wrong?'

His response left me speechless! 'I'm not sure I'm doing the right thing,' he said, wringing his hands.

I sat looking at the misery on his face. 'Is it because of the family?'

'Don't know. It's just a feeling I have in the pit of my stomach that won't let go.'

Maybe this is just a groom's typical nerves, I hoped.

The following morning I was thankful Darlene and her Nottingham friends were staying at another location nearby, unaware of the drama about to unfold at our breakfast table. As the two of us sat toying with teaspoons in our hands, from the look on his face, I knew breakfast would not appeal to him. His right hand waved from right to left, left to right, until finally I urged, 'What is the matter?'

'Not sure I can go through with it,' was the blunt reply.

'Bit late for that, isn't it?' I said, feeling a nauseous shadow engulf me. 'How do you think the bride's going to feel, if you back out?'

'What's more,' I added, 'William, it's your life. If you are thinking of your children, forget it. Do they really care? Remember how you and Darlene were shunned when you announced your engagement to her and they refused point blank to attend your reception?'

Thinking it might calm him down, I offered him a cup of strong sweet tea. This was a brother I dearly loved and to see him going through such agony, tore at my heart. I took a piece of toast off a plate on the dining table and as I sat eating, my eyes never left his face as if to question, 'What will you do?'

He finished drinking his tea then rose from the dining table, saying, 'I'm going to get dressed.'

Time was running short, so I hurriedly ate the last piece of toast and left the table, then went to the bathroom to wash and change from a housecoat into my new outfit for the wedding. Hearing not a peep from William since breakfast, I assumed the wedding was still on. Spruced up and "ready to kill", I went in the living room and saw William standing, staring out of the window, looking smartly dressed in a new grey suit. We hugged, as though for the last time.

'Ready to go?'

We were about to lock the door of the apartment, when Daniel walked in. I whispered, 'Have you the ring?'

He nodded.

The limousine taking us to the registry office arrived well ahead of time and at the bequest of the driver who held open the side door for us, we climbed in and sat in the back seat. As we drove toward Farnham, black clouds skirted across a grey sky, threatening a heavy fall of rain.

Convincing myself it won't rain today, the sun will shine, I held tight to William's arm. Smiling at him, with a "chin up" look of encouragement, we entered through the registry office door. Once seated with his son to one side of him and his sister on the other side, and among friends, I hoped he wouldn't turn tail back home.

Although it was painful to William that his daughter and younger son were adamant not to attend his wedding, he remained silent on the matter for some considerable time, long after the wedding. There was little in the way of comfort anyone could offer, to ease a seemingly irreconcilable situation. Darlene's philosophy of their attitude toward her appeared blasé. As she was often to quote: 'people have choices.'

I was happy the marriage ceremony went well. William appeared more relaxed, now the waiting was over. Like all brides, Darlene looked radiant in her new cream colour outfit and matching hat.

Months later, the animosity towards her by his family increased threefold. Having come a long way in her life bringing up three children alone, after her young husband passed away, Darlene told William in no uncertain term the snubbed treatment was unwarranted from his family, and was more than she could bear. With reluctance, she left him and went back up north. A gregarious person who loved to dance, sing and laugh, of a generous nature, I thought she was the perfect partner for my brother. More in tune to William's character who forever wanted to keep to the world spinning round, as they heartily shared jokes and never stopped laughing.

The marriage was on a slippery slope from the beginning. The night before the wedding when most grooms are out celebrating, William was home struggling with the uncertainty of whether to go through with his marriage to Darlene or not. He did not want to let go of the fact that a daughter whom he dearly loved and a younger son who visited him frequently after working hours, would no longer visit. But the die was cast. There was no turning back the clock.

One concern I had for my brother was the sheer misery his family had caused him. Losing a caring mother was understandable in the eyes of his children, and reason enough for them not to accept a stranger in their midst from the north of the country, but to take an instant dislike to a person they did not wish to know or even try to get to know, went beyond understanding. In their minds, future financial gains from their father would go to his wife, rather than to them. The marriage could have worked had the couple been able to enjoy a lifestyle without family interference. Their father having supported them financially before and after their own marriages, and to be treated in this fashion, their narrow-mindedness left me incapable of words.

On many occasions I sensed William's regret he did not hold on to Darlene, as he spoke of her in endearing words and told me they rang each other weekly.

ROUGH AND WOOLLY

My yearly visits to William continued with much anticipation. On our two weeks stay at the Crown we had no intention of remaining or milling with the hotel visitors, but spent each awakening day touring different parts of Dorset. From Weymouth Bay the sandy shores stretched for miles along the coastline to Portland Bill, Chesil Beach and the fishing town of Lyme Regis.

Many stories related from the locals deemed it a "necessary evil" when Allied armies, navy and air force took the county of Dorset by surprise, with its heavy artillery in the quiet English countryside (some American equipment even today stands rusting in farmland fields) and naval bases that prohibited the public from using the beaches by stretching its perimeter with spiky barbed wire. During World War Two, Allied ships convoyed from Chesil Beach, a strategic point for naval reconnaissance. The surrounding areas were heavily barricaded, to keep friend or foe from entering a restricted area.

On trips to Portland Bill, at whatever time or day we visited strong winds blew off the English channel, sending up plumes of white spray over the rocks and shoreline. The angry ocean did not invite one to dive in and swim. Each gust of wind forced high waves to splash over the heavy boulders where we stood courageously facing the wind as it

William at Selsey Bill.

howled through our thin jackets, often soaking us if we were too close to the edge of the cliff. "Rough and Woolly" is how we viewed the scene, as we looked down to a sheer rocky drop of 100 feet or more, from above.

Dorchester, on the Frome River, 50 miles WSW of Southampton, has many old-world pubs where we lunched and dined. Its ancient history goes back a long way. The 15th-century church contains the tombs of many well-known celebrities. Thomas Hardy of *Wessex* novels lived in a thatched cottage at Dorchester that is open to the public on certain weekdays. The weekly farmer's market is a place to chat, lunch, and search for the perfect bargain. Or, as many housewives in the district were known to do, gossip about one another, until the cows came home. A day's outing for most, it gave them the opportunity to dawdle in time, and meet old and new friends.

The property at Waterlooville was smaller than the one at Crookhorn, but equally well-furnished and situated conveniently near a bus route, to reach the town. A small variety shop close by, run by an East Indian family whose one aim was to please all customers, sold all and sundry. Since it took less time and energy to walk there from his home, William bought newspapers and cigarettes from the shop, to the delight of the owners. A packet of cigarettes costing twenty-five pounds sterling, gave William the status of being a worthy customer.

Normally, when going into Portsmouth to shop, I took the bus. William, on the other hand, if he wanted to go into town and pop into the bookie's to place his bets, hired a taxi. I sensed he had an aversion to crowds on buses and wondered if taking a taxi gave him more time to mull over the horses running at a certain race course, that day. Perhaps taking this route gave him an edge to feel slightly superior to his betting cronies. Whichever reason he chose, I simply tagged along, listening to William gush forth non-stop with tips to the taxi driver.

On one such occasion, a young driver picked us up and appeared full of nervous energy. As he drove out of the driveway I almost jumped out of my seat when he shouted, 'I won, I won!'

Unable to hold back his curiosity, William asked, 'Which horse?'

'A tip you gave me on a filly running the 2:30 p.m. at Doncaster, with a funny name. I put two quids on a bet, twenty to one.'

I could hear William sniff, as his mathematical mind quickly calculated the winnings. Facing the driver, 'You did well,' he said casually.

Looking ahead at the road in front of him, our young driver laughed, 'Can you give us another tip?'

One day William locked the front door of his home, and turned cautiously to walk down the six wide concrete steps to reach the road. Looking up at the sky, with black clouds looming across, he knew it would not be long before the heavens opened. Walking in hurried strides along the pavement, he hoped to reach the variety shop and pick up his daily newspaper before the clouds burst. As he pushed open the door to the shop the owner, a man in his early forties with black hair, of medium height, and a smile that stretched from ear to ear, walked towards him. Clasping his hands together as though to keep them warm, he asked if there was something he could get for his customer. I cannot begin to imagine the reaction on the face of the owner when William announced all he needed was his newspaper.

'No cigarettes today?' asked the owner, blandly. The smile no longer on his face, his hands hanging limp down each side of his body. William shook his head. To put the owner out of his misery, he then told him on the advice of his doctor he was not allowed to smoke, with a warning, 'One more cigarette, end of story.'

As he walked home with the newspaper tucked safely under one arm, William wondered who of the two was sorrier, the shopkeeper or himself.

The following months he struggled to deal with withdrawal symptoms in an effort to give up smoking, and failed miserably. His happy-go-lucky nature ebbed to its lowest point. His betting cronies, noting the change, urged him to go back on cigarettes and let the consequences take care of itself.

On his next visit to the doctor William sat in a chair opposite him, with a dog-look expression on his face, as he tried to explain why he was feeling so depressed. After listening, the doctor curtly remarked, 'If it makes you that miserable, go back on them. But cut back on the number you smoke. A large package a week is far too many.'

William was on cloud nine and returned home in a much lighter mood, but still had doubts chasing inside his head if he should do as the doctor suggested. Entering his living room he sat in a deep leather chair and listened to the big clock over the fireplace ticking louder and louder, causing him to take action when the big hand hit the appointed hour. Reaching to where his telephone sat on a side table, close to his chair, he lifted it off its cradle and dialled his son-in-law's number. Hearing his voice at the end of the line, William asked, 'Can you come over? Yes, right now?'

Before his son-in-law had the chance to refuse, William said, in a flat voice, 'I don't smoke any more. You can come and take the rest of my cigarettes.'

When I first heard the story how my brother gave up smoking, to be able to quit "cold-turkey" after puffing on cigarettes for years, it truly astonished me!

Our bracing days at Portland Bill continued, with on-going interest at the sheer magnitude of the cold and unrelenting channel that dared anyone to challenge its ferocity. The weather, be it springtime or summertime, it either drizzled rain and if the sun ever managed to get through the clouds, the shine was weak to the point its rays gave little warmth. A wind burn was another matter, if one chose to stand and watch and listen as the ocean roared, causing the waves to splash high above the rocks. A visitor could tolerate this exposure but for a short time. To stand too close to the edge of the cliff was to invite a soaking.

Gulls and other sea birds, conditioned to its thermostatic climes, soared high above the shoreline and dipped wings to the rhythm of the waves.

The thrill of seeing the wonders of nature's landscape at its best and at its worse will be etched in our memories of Portland Bill as "Rough and Woolly".

CULINARY SKILLS

William's culinary skills were, to say the least, unorthodox. Watching him balance a small tray on the kitchen scales as he weighed ingredients for a large fruit cake, flour, sugar, butter, eggs, dried fruit, spices and liquids, all unceremoniously went in a large mixing bowl. With a long handle wooden spoon he stirred the ingredients until they blended enough to drop off the spoon, when shaken.

This method of baking a cake often left me too speechless for words as it contradicted every lesson in the cookery books, but I never questioned William's ability to produce a perfectly-baked fruit cake. What was more remarkable when the cake was removed from the oven, it turned out flawless. No fruit sinking in the middle. No burnt edges. Just perfect!

At one time, however, I decided to take the "plunge" and bake a cake exactly the same way he did. To say I was horrified when removing the cake from the oven, would be the understatement of the year. I could have cried for wasting good ingredients. The cake had sunk in the middle, and was as heavy as lead. I could barely hold onto the baking tin, when lifting it out of the oven – an experience I was not about to repeat.

With four granddaughters and three grandsons living close by,

William cheerfully baked all their birthday cakes. I never heard a criticism from anyone about the texture or quality. Of course no member of the family would dream of asking him what method he used to bake a fruit cake. Once sliced and handed round the dining table, the cake disappeared in record time. All much to the delight of William who never sampled a piece, but sat smiling as teeth, young and old, munched on each slice until nothing but crumbs were left on the plate. Perhaps it was the supreme marzipan and icing on top, that quelled the taste buds when eating the birthday cake. But, in essence, it was a gift of love.

I happened to recall to my brother a cake experience way back when food of any kind in the 1940s was at arm's length, unless you had pockets of hard-earned money and were able to afford black market prices for any additional rations. But it wasn't the black market most of my factory colleagues went for. Instead we biked from Walton-on-Thames, Surrey to Kingston where an American army base was stationed at Bushy Park and the girls wasted little time sorting out the good from the bad food dumped in boxes outside the camp, for the taking. We were like rats and mice scurrying here, there and everywhere not to miss anything that looked remotely edible.

With my share of the booty of a box of currants, and other goodies, and Christmas round the corner, I headed for home. Next day, after work, full of enthusiastic energy with the prospects of baking a perfect cake, I set to with whatever ingredients I had, using a recipe by the well-known English cook Mrs. Beeton, going back to the early 1920s, and put the cake in a two-pound size pan to bake in a slow oven. The required three hours to bake a fruit cake seemed too long a time for me to sit up and wait. Thinking I had earned a rest after working all day, I went upstairs to lie on my bed. Hours later, I awoke to the smell of baking, which caused me to hurry downstairs and run into the kitchen. The odour from the oven hit my nostrils, with alarm. I opened the oven door and knew before I lifted the cake pan off the rack, King Alfred the Great would acclaim first prize before I ever would. It was burnt to a cinder.

On one visit to William he surprised me when he invited Elizabeth and me to dinner at the local golf club to celebrate my birthday. Having eaten a substantial meal, wined and dined, it was a complete surprise when a waitress came into the private room he had booked for the occasion, to see her put an iced cake on the table. I looked at Elizabeth who said naught, then at William, who gave a wide grin.

'You two,' I said, 'know how to surprise one.'

I knew my sister had previously been warned by him of the intended birthday cake.

'Who iced the cake?' I asked, knowing full well it was William.

Holding a glass of whiskey between thumb and finger, 'Happy birthday', he laughed. I thanked him with a peck on the cheek.

One day I was watching William making a birthday cake and asked if I ever mentioned a particular episode in my husband's life, when he was a child.

'No, can't remember you ever telling me about it,' he said, with complete concentration on the job at hand, as he busily stirred in the dried fruit with a long wooden handle in a large mixing bowl on the kitchen table. Casting one eye in my direction, the other eye on the work at hand, I proceeded with my story about my Welsh Connection.

THE WELSH CONNECTION

To his one attentive ear, I related to William the episode of a ten-year-old blond boy known as Clarence. His Grandmother Harris, of medium height, long black hair coiled at the back of her head held tight with pins, was an excellent organist and played at all her local church services. Some of her neighbours furtively gossiped she was a clairvoyant.

Clasping young Clarence to her large bosom, gently stroking his head, she asked him to take his first cousin Kay, a six-year-old blonde, to the local fish and chip shop a block away from where she lived, and buy the family's dinner. It was a regular scene in the chip shop when other families in the neighbourhood were eager to smell and eat fish and chips as they stood in line at the counter, waiting to be served. Gossip ran rife with ladies wearing rollers on their heads, colourful aprons over their frocks, as they inhaled the steamy atmosphere of oil cooking cod, plaice, haddock and hake fried to each customer's choice.

Withdrawing the money from his pocket, Clarence placed it on the top of the counter. The owner checked for the correct amount of pennies then handed him his order of fish and chips, wrapped in newspaper. Carefully holding his family's dinner he felt the heat through the newspaper, and saw grease oozing from the folded sheets. As the cousins were walking home, the heat coming off the newspaper gradually cooled. The smell of the food, however, caused young Kay to bite hard on her lips. Distracting Clarence's attention, she pushed two small fingers of her right hand sneakily into the folds of the newspaper, and took out a couple of chips, making sure her head was turned away from him as she ate them. By the time the pair reached home, Grandma Harris, upon opening the newspaper to take out the food, was shocked to the bones as she laid out the few chips on a serving platter. The fish was intact. All that remained of her order from the fish and chip shop, to feed her family of eight, had diminished in size, greatly.

'Crafty kid,' said my brother, as he continued mixing fruit ingredients in the large bowl. 'Well,' he added, 'I guess she got a well-deserved clip round the ear for that?'

'No,' I replied in an effort to keep the momentum flowing. 'Because she brazenly blamed Clarence for eating the missing chips. Widening her innocent blue eyes wider at Grandmother, Kay was not the culprit.'

It left Grandmother scurrying to the pantry to rustle up whatever food was left so the family could enjoy a meal of a sort, including the fish. The few chips, now cold, were put on Grandfather's plate.

On another occasion, the cousins were sent to the local bakery. Grandma's two strong hands painstakingly mixed flour, yeast, sugar and water to a pliable dough, enough to make four loaves of bread. The dough, shaped into medium-sized loaves, was put on tin trays and covered with kitchen cloths. Handing one tray to Clarence with a warning, 'Bring them back untouched and don't steal, otherwise you know where God will send you. Burn in Hell.' He took the tray from her, hoping his Saviour from above would whisper in his cousin's ear, not to steal the family's food.

Alas, the warning went unheeded.

Clarence held on tight to his tray, and gave his Grandmother a look as if to say, 'I'm not the greedy one.'

Returning home, each child carried a tray holding two freshly-baked loaves of bread. Despite the heavenly smell permeating from beneath the cloth, Clarence would not be tempted to sample a crumb. It pleased his grandmother when she saw how well her loaves turned out. Penny a piece, to bake at the local bakery, was food for the soul. Taking the tray holding the other two loaves from Kay, Grandmother knew before she peeped beneath the white cloth, who was the guilty one. Checking each loaf, the girl kept her eyes on Grandmother's stern face. While awaiting the verdict, she fidgeted and shifted one foot to the other. The tell-tale signs of desperate fingers poking holes in the crust at both ends of each loaf, was evident enough.

'Well, my girl,' reprimanded Grandmother, 'no supper for you'.

Family members sitting around the long scrubbed kitchen table waiting for tea to be served, wholeheartedly agreed. A thief is not worthy of Grandmother's hard work in providing food for her family. In their eyes, to steal was bad enough, but to steal from one's own relatives, an unforgivable sin.

'No, no treat for the greedy,' said one and all in unison. 'She's had her share of chips and crusts of bread.'

'And to think we blamed young Clarence,' one sister squeaked to the other.

It was evident the back room of the miner's house, kept comfortably warm with the fireplace lit night and day, is where the family took long-drawn-out meals at the large scrubbed kitchen table. All were oblivious to the sound of the big oak clock hanging on the kitchen wall, ticking away the hours, as they exchanged local gossip.

These houses were built of brick in terraces and often looked drab outside, but inside were sparkling clean. They belonged to the companies who owned the mines, one of the main industries in the Clydach area, and provided them at a low rent. The miners were given a monthly allowance of coal and coke, fuel to keep their houses warm. This was their only form of heat. No bathrooms or running hot water were in any of the homes. Buckets or large aluminium tubs were used for laundry and taking baths.

I came into that family fold when Clarence Whitehead and I married in the mid-forties. He was a twenty-three-year-old, six-foot handsome man with blond hair and broad shoulders akin to those of his Derbyshire ancestors, noted for their stocky build and dry sense of humour. During the summer months we made a point to visit his family in South Wales, a place where I had never been. At my first introduction I was extremely shy when meeting his close-knit family and realized in order to become accepted as one of them, I needed to show what skills I had as a young housewife to manage the running of a household. But how would I do that?

My husband was stationed at the army barracks in County Durham in the north of England and would shortly be due home on leave. He was in the Royal Engineers. Travelling from north of the country to the south of London where his parents and I currently lived was a tiring journey, by train.

Food was still rationed and were it not for the fact my father-in-law grew many of his own vegetables in his long, narrow garden plot, as well as breeding angora rabbits to provide us with meat, the variety of food on the table would be restricted by the number of weekly food coupons available. Two pork chops didn't go far, especially during the cooking process when they sizzled down to half their size.

With a large black cooking pot, in went the skinned, cut up rabbit, onions and every vegetable from the garden. I wanted to time and cook it perfectly, to coincide with the arrival of my soldier husband. Waiting patiently in the kitchen at the end of the hall while keeping an eye on the rabbit stew, a cold draft hit my face as the front door of the house suddenly flew open. There was my husband. His mother was first in line to greet him, then a handshake from his father. I thought my shoes had glued to the red linoleum on the hallway floor, as I couldn't move. Instead of the anticipated passionate kiss on the lips, my husband came over and gave me a hug. Perhaps this lack of adoration was because his aunt and her daughter were also standing inside the door, to watch his first homecoming.

We all sat down at the dining table to enjoy the first rabbit stew I had

Four-year-old Clive.

ever made. After taking one or two mouthfuls of food, I wasn't sure how the rest of the family would react to the meal placed before them. I put my fork down on the table and with a questioning expression on my face, asked my husband if he thought the food tasted sweet.

'Does a bit. Perhaps it's the carrots,' he said, smiling.

It wasn't until the rest of the family commented about the food being too sweet, did I replace it with bread and cheese, and a pot of tea, and learn it was young Kay who had ruined the stew. To add further insult to injury, when pressured, she owned up to putting the precious little sugar we had left in the kitchen tin in the rabbit pot. Then she further reduced our ration supplies by lacing the tea with salt. I was mortified. What

I hoped would create an ever-lasting impression on my husband's first homecoming, turned out a disaster.

When the family questioned, 'Why?' the girl simply shrugged her small shoulders.

Kay's younger brother Clive was different to his sister as chalk and cheese, and lived a few houses away in the same street as my in-laws. Whenever I saw him playing outside in the road he reminded me of one of Dickens' urchins in *"Oliver Twist"*. The boy always looked half-starved, wore baggy second-hand shorts below the knees and often as not, wore no shoes. His light brown hair was unkempt and like straw. His face never appeared to be washed. Compared to his sister, he was a friendly little boy with an impish grin that made me want to hug him and bring him into my in-law's kitchen and give whatever food we had, if only a chunk of freshly-baked bread and tinned jam.

I'm not sure where this jam was made, or came from, but it had to be the worst jam in the history of culinary delicacies. It didn't taste like any particular fruit, regardless of the label describing it as strawberry, plum, or any other kind. However, after the war it became common knowledge this preserve barely consisted of any fruit at all; the basic ingredients were root vegetables, mainly turnips. It did not surprise the housewife when hearing this, knowing how difficult it was when using a spoon to scoop the jam out of a tin or jar, it was not jam at all.

Clive and his little friends from the neighbourhood often played away from home and walked two or three miles to the Walton-on-Thames railway station. On a hot summer day, four boys casually strolled to the station, chatting all the way without pause. When they reached the station the four jumped over the concrete platform and landed on the rail tracks. Laughing and straddling between the ruts on thin, short legs, they played catch-me-if-you-can. Hearing the rumble of a distant noise, Clive's friends ran for safety and clambered back over the concrete platform. Clive did not heed the warning in time, as the on-coming train slammed into him. He was six years old.

In the early years of my marriage to Clarence, I asked William, 'When next on shore leave, will you accompany Elizabeth and myself to meet the Welsh side of the family?'

Surprisingly, he said, 'Yes.'

I daresay at the back of his mind he was curious to know what sort of people they were and if all he had heard about the Welsh people, was true or false. Great singers, yes. Coal miners he admired, but had never met. So a trip was planned for the Autumn.

A sure sign the weather was changing with cooling temperatures, was when the leaves on the trees in Kensington Gardens turned bright red, rust and yellow and then gradually shed their cloak of Autumn colours. As the evenings began to draw in and the sun faded into a distant sky, a light mist, known as Scotch mist, shrouded the surrounding landscape. This type of mist, or blanket of fogs, known as "pea soup", was particularly evident in many parts of London due to the large numbers of chimney pots that stood on rooftops belching out coal fumes. Fogs or mists hung like spider webs over tall buildings standing between narrow streets, cautioning the traveller to cling tight to the edge or sides of the building through a blurry vision.

When my sister and I took evening strolls in Kensington Gardens during the Autumn months, the dampness of the mist caused us to wrap our coats up and over our necks to avoid the moisture creeping in. To venture in the park without wearing a hat not only invited a head cold, but a cold head.

The day before the Wales trip when William joined us at Elizabeth's flat, it was warm and sunny. His normal way of arriving at the flat was by taxi. Hearing the slamming of a car door, Elizabeth and I went and opened the front door to him and watched as he generously tipped the driver. The three of us went back inside, happy to spend time together. Elizabeth's first suggestion: a cup of tea. The following morning we awoke to the sound of rain pelting down on the windows. The temperature had fallen sharply overnight, and the flat was so cold it made us shiver.

After breakfast, a taxi took us to Paddington Station and from there we caught the train going through the counties of Oxfordshire, Gloucestershire and Cardiff, to Glamorganshire. Sitting in a third-class carriage we chatted non-stop the full length of the journey, speaking to the rhythm of the wheels rattling along the tracks. When the train reached Cardiff we left the railway station and headed to the nearest pub for lunch, before continuing our journey by bus to the Rhonda Valley.

'I'll have a quickie,' said William, rubbing his hands to warm up, as he headed to the bar.

I thought he meant he'd shoot around the back of the bar to the toilet. But no, he went up to the bar, put his elbow on the counter, and ordered a double whiskey. The barman looked at him, as though in shock! A group of old men sitting in a corner by the open fireplace gazed with large eyes, observing this stranger who sauntered into their sanctuary to order a quickie.

Downing the whiskey in record time, William asked the shocked barman for another.

One of the men in the group whispered to the others, 'Man, must be a wealthy foreigner, drinking four whiskeys in one go.'

But, taking no further interest in the stranger holding up the bar, the group carried on chatting and drinking.

The valleys extending north from the Bristol Channel are: Rhonda, Ebbw Vale, Merthyr Tydfil, Mountain Ash and Pontypridd. Rhonda, in central Glamorgan, 19 miles NW of Cardiff, was the coal-mining and steel-mining centre.

Merthyr's history goes back to 1066 when the Normans came to Britain and occupied South Wales. Because the area was so wild, seldom was Merthyr visited. The first iron furnace was established in 1757. Due to the findings of coal and iron deposits, the area grew rapidly. As its industries grew, so did its population.

Over the years when visiting the area, I found it a depressing sight. A ghost town. You could smell its history. Everything looked sooty. Old mining wheels stood silent on top of deserted shafts that no longer hummed with human beings coming and going all hours of the night and day in pits, black as the coal embedded in them. Although the mines were closed for a number of years, the air hung heavy with remnants of coal dust; the whole atmospheric neighbourhood and surrounding villages, left one trembling. It is impossible to understand the appalling conditions of the miners who suffered injuries and death working in the underground shafts so they could eke out a wage barely sufficient to support their families.

In the pub we sat at a table chatting while we ate lunch, occasionally pausing to listen to the Welsh dialect around us. Furtive glances from those we assumed to be retired miners, caused us to feel we were intruders and had no right being there. But one pauses to consider this an odd assumption, due to the fact Cardiff Chamber of Commerce welcomed visitors with open arms in their promotional magazine. I was, however, thankful William had discarded his P.O. uniform for civilian clothes on this particular visit, as I could foresee "a clap of thunder" had he not done so. It was simply an odd feeling on my part!

Road signs in Welsh did not come about until after the Second World War. Today, the traveller who does not understand or speak the Welsh language would find himself driving up the wrong mountains and down the misty-glazed valleys which could take him miles off the beaten track.

To William and Elizabeth I recalled my first visit to Wales, and how there was some consternation on a freezing cold night in December, when my husband was driving the car to spend Christmas with his family in the Rhonda Valley. We found ourselves going farther and farther up an unknown mountain that didn't show on our map, and took us almost back to our starting point at the Welsh border. Stopping at the first garage, we asked the Welsh mechanic for directions. He was a man of medium height, who looked about the age of thirty years. He stood languidly wiping his greasy hands on his overalls, while listening to a our tale of woe.

'Crikey.' The word stretched a mile and a half out of his mouth. 'You're miles off track,' he laughed.

Looking about him, with our tired bodies ready to drop, he pointed to where we should go to get us back on the right road. After we thanked the mechanic for his help, he watched as we turned the car round and descended the mountain through the cover of a flimsy mist. Once back on the right road it was all we could do to suppress our laughter at his melodious accent; it was one we had never heard before.

In the early hours of dawn, mountain sheep were already on the move tipping over dustbins for early breakfast. It drizzled rain. It was perishingly cold!

After knocking on the front door of a miner's terraced brick house which extended from the top to the end of Clydach Road, Grandmother Harris opened the door, a look of concern on her face. 'Heavens above, where have you been?'

Too exhausted to give an explanation Clarence and I begged for a cup of tea, and bed.

From the day I met this kindly lady, she was always immaculately dressed. With every hair on her head in place, and wearing a spotless white apron over a long black skirt, her presence held me in awe. Her tight-knit family, however, did not readily encourage into their midst strangers, who held their breath when meeting them for the first time, knowing they were thoroughly scrutinized, before being accepted.

Her husband, William Harris, was a strong-minded character and one did not cross his path willingly, without reason. He barely deemed it worthwhile to put a smile on his face. Yet his son Tom of the same build, same red hair and bushy eyebrows, also a miner, but often gave belly laughs that were contagious to the point all around him joined in. Perhaps some were even not sure what they were laughing about in the first place.

I should not have been so concerned when introducing Grandmother to my brother, but my heart was in my mouth as he and my sister were visiting Wales for the first time. Fervently, I hoped William would not be too gregarious in his introduction to the family, as they sat tight-lipped at the kitchen table as though waiting to pass judgement.

Elizabeth, with her tender nature and soft smile, invited strangers of all kind to take notice of her. Uncle Tom rose from the table and offered her his seat. Eight sat down at the table to a meal of beets, onions, eggs in pickled jars, cold ham, freshly-baked bread, Welsh cakes and a variety of tartlets, served on antique plates. Savouring mouthfuls of food, and listening to the bubble of voices that sounded melodious to the point of singing, I chose to listen rather than chat. Early evening the men left the ladies to go off to the nearest pub, where a stage was set-up for a singing contest. I wondered if William would have the nerve to take the bait.

My sister and I offered to clear the table and help wash the plates in the scullery near the back door, but Grandmother would not hear of it. We suspected she didn't want us catching a chill by standing on the lop-sided flagstones on the damp floor. The scullery was dark and cold; even mice scurried along. Next to the scullery was a pantry where ham or pork joints hung on steel hooks from wooden beams. These were purchased from one of the local farms, along with rabbits and hares, by Grandfather Harris who was friendly with many of the farmers. Supplies of meat relied heavily on Grandfather's wins at the race course where he and his friend Dr. Watson went every Saturday to Cardiff or another race course close by, come rain or shine.

During this period of his life, Grandfather ran a small grocery shop. With his winnings at the race course, he purchased cases of Carnation tinned milk most Welsh housewives used for tea instead of milk, as it was cheaper to buy. I was unaware of this part of his character and deemed somewhere in that hard heart of his there was an atom of sympathy, for those less fortunate than himself. In his generous arrangement with local neighbours who bought the tinned milk from him and couldn't quite afford to pay for it on a weekly basis, he allowed them credit, and to pay when monies became available. In so doing, all his winnings were lost on bad debts and finally he was forced to close the shop, putting it down to hard times and a bad experience. There were not many murmurs from those he treated well who were the cause of his downfall, and who edged away from him to find other means of buying and bartering for tinned milk.

On wooden shelves, heavy earthenware containers held a variety of home-made wines – parsnip, dandelion, elderberry, rhubarb and blackberry waiting to ferment and be bottled. Heady stuff! Too much taken at any one time had one spewing up, and nursing a splitting headache. Several earthenware jars held home-grown vegetables laid between salt, others preserved fruits. Some of the produce was bought from local farms at harvest time, when supplies were abundant. Welsh housewives knew the value of preserving food, cooking and baking in black stone ovens, stews simmering in big pots on top of hot plates, heated by coke, to keep their families fed. A Celtic race, who can survive in any storm!

With every visit to Wales, my admiration for the miners grew in leaps and bounds. Although I did not understand their culture nor indeed their language, I fully understood how they remained, from birth to death, close-knit families. Once accepted by them, their kindness is overwhelming.

Elizabeth and I retired early to bed, unaware of the time at night the men returned home from the pub. We had no idea if William managed to get to his bed and breakfast, previously booked in Tonypandy, close by. Neither did we inquire the following day, at noon, when we saw him sitting at the kitchen table holding his head in his hands.

I asked Elizabeth how she slept. 'Well, not bad really, but I heard the banging of lids during the early hours of dawn.'

My father-in-law, whom I dearly loved and called Pop, was sitting in a kitchen chair listening to the conversation round him, puffed on his smelly pipe. I'm not sure what type tobacco he put in his briar pipe to burn, but the smell was awful. Enough to make one gag!

'Can't get away with that, any night,' he said in a strong north country accent, looking at Elizabeth with a broad grin. 'The sheep come down from the mountains to raid the dustbins for whatever scraps of food they can find to eat. Some nights you would think thunder was raging across the moors.'

The Welsh cultural life has given us The National Eisteddford, the annual festival with actors, poets, playwrights, singers, musicians and male voice choirs, all performing in the Welsh language.

A native of Wales, whose poems are greatly respected for their simplicity, W.H. Davies was born in 1871 at Monmouthshire. He was related to the famous British actor Sir Henry Irving. An unbeliever, in his philosophical mind studying academics was considered time wasted. Instead he became a vagabond, tramping round the counties of England, the provinces of Canada and the United States of America. His poem *"What is this life, if full of care, we have no time to stop and stare"* was published 1911.

Another of his poems entitled *"The Fog"* was published 1913. *"A blind man leads the poet through the fog, tells the reader that one who is handicapped in one domain may well have a considerable advantage in another."* The words of Davies clearly define his writings of the joys and sorrows of human nature and how it affected his life as a tramp.

In due course we left Cardiff and headed back to London, by train. Watching the scenery flash by, and listening to the regular clackety-clack of the wheels searing against the tracks, William and Elizabeth appeared deep in thought. Giving him a slight prod in the ribs, I asked, 'How did you enjoy your visit to Wales, and your night in the pub where a singing concert was held?'

'Good. And can't those Welsh sing!' he responded in a tired voice, as though still getting over his hangover at the pub.

'Did you get up on the stage to sing?' I asked.

'I'm not telling.'

Conversation between the three of us was at a lull. It looked as though any minute, we would all be sound asleep. When the whistle sounded and the train puffed its way into the station we took our luggage off the overhead rack, ready to leave the carriage when the train came to a full stop at Paddington.

Outside the railway station William hailed a taxi to take us to Kensington. When we arrived, he asked the driver if he could wait a second or two. After saying goodbye to Elizabeth and seeing her safely inside her flat, we went back in the taxi and headed to Waterloo Station where we caught our train going southbound. Once seated in the carriage William appeared more alert, and began chatting up a storm about his first visit to Wales. His comments of the family were not all positive but their being close-knit and how they survived many hardships, impressed him.

All too soon the train chugged its way into Walton-on-Thames Station where I said goodbye to him, as I stepped down from the train onto the platform. William continued his journey to Hampshire and stayed with his family for two days, before returning to Portsmouth where his ship was docked and due to sail the next morning.

It would be two years before Elizabeth and I were to see him again. Instead of arriving at his usual shore base, Portsmouth, his ship docked at Lowestoft near Great Yarmouth, bordering close to the North Sea, "a freezing hole" he dreaded. Having spent months in the warmer climes of Gibraltar and Malta, the dampness of the English climate seeped through him. The journey from Lowestoft took longer for him to reach his family at Cosham. However he considered all things being equal, when seafaring men took it in their stride and travelled in groups on trains with camaraderie in full swing, it made the long journey appear shorter.

LEG OF LAMB

The children were growing up fast. The two boys were the proud owners of bicycles bought with money they had earned themselves, and often cycled into town to pick up the odd grocery item for their mother. Amanda continued to cling to her mother's apron, giving the impression she was about to drown in a swirling river. Thinking she needed more freedom from the home, Violet felt the urge to take up something of interest, anything, to fulfil her modest needs. When she discussed this with William he encouraged her to go ahead and see what was available in the work force, where perhaps she could make new friends. He was of the opinion that a woman wasn't born to be tied to the kitchen sink.

With William's support Violet wasted little time applying to the local school to take on any task offered. She became a "lolly pop" lady. Holding up the traffic with her long stick, with a red stop sign at the top of it, she guided the children to the other side of the road until they were safely across. Some of the pupils coming out of school were cheeky. Violet took her new duties seriously and when some of the young lads tested her patience by purposely dawdling as she tried to get them safely across the road, a slight twitch developed in one of her eyes. One nine-year-old boy with red hair wore glasses too big. His daily repertoire never failed: 'Any lolly pops today, Miss?' as he ran to the other side of the road, giggling.

Violet revelled in her new role. She was popular with the staff and school children as well as her co-workers, whom she met often on weekends at a cafe for coffee or for a cuppa in the afternoon. William was pleased with the change in his wife, who smiled and joked about the day's event. Her dry sense of humour was now more evident, as she described the high jinks from some of the school lads.

Showing Elizabeth and I her new motorized two-wheel scooter and how to ride it, Violet sat on the rubber seat, looking relaxed. Turning the key in a small slot on the dashboard, the scooter putt-putted softly down the road, in near-silent wonder! The look on the face of my sister-in-law was of sheer bliss.

Despite his good skills as an engineer, William never thought it necessary to become the driver of a car. I didn't asked why, although was tempted to do so on several occasions. I had the impression he liked someone driving him to wherever he wanted to go, rather than steer behind the wheel. I can imagine the hundreds of pounds he had spent over the years, using taxis to get from A to B, visiting Dorset and other parts of the west coast, with fares over one hundred pounds. If I had raised an eyebrow, I am sure I would have been politely told: 'Don't worry.'

Early July 1980, I stayed a few days with Elizabeth at her flat in West Kensington. We took evening strolls in the sunlit gardens nearby, and stopped to admire the different plants and shrubs. Checking for any sign of a herbal plant I said, 'Too bad there is no rosemary bush or mint among them.'

I made this comment knowing my sister intended buying a leg of lamb for dinner and had invited William to stay overnight on the Saturday, and share Sunday's meal with us.

Macey's butcher shop – no longer standing – was located off one of the side streets, one block from where my sister lived. A family-run business going back to the reign of Queen Victoria, over the years, it was handed down from father to son. A yellow and blue striped awning hung over the entrance of the shop door. Its bright colours swayed in the wind as it gusted across the side street, enticing customers to enter. With constant cleaning the shop windows inside and outside sparkled, and often caused customers to stop and mirror a face in them.

Jack Macey purchased his meats from the Covent Garden market in London. With an eye for quality, he served nothing but the best for his customers. The market not only sold meat, but fruits, vegetables and flowers. It opened at the crack of dawn and if a tradesman didn't get there before 5 a.m., to his chagrin, the pickings were slim. It was a place where tradespeople gathered to hear family gossip or exchange business news or daily events. Also an opportune time for some to stop for a quickie at one of the pubs, before heading home. After his customary farewell, with his purchases in the back of his van, and the hope of making quick sales, Jack returned home.

Like most butchers who fed off the fat of the land, Jack Macey was a solidly-built man of medium height and had a healthy, ruddy complexion. A true Londoner, his sense of humour never wavered. He served each customer with a hearty smile, often stopping with the customer's order held in his hand as he inquired about their family. His wife Nancy and her two sons, Tim and John, lived in the flat above the shop. On Saturday afternoons the boys helped with carving slices off the cured ham that sat on a marble slab on top a wooden bench, and placed the slices on a china platter, ready to be served. They were also expected to earn their weekly allowance by cleaning up the counter tops and sweeping the floor after the shop closed. Nancy took care of the big brown glazed earthenware pots that stood either side of the shop entrance, and replaced the old flowers with fresh ones bought from Covent Garden, as they died off.

We picked up a leg of lamb at Macey's , then went to the greengrocer to buy fresh vegetables. Carrying them back to the flat, with the weight of the supplies, I wondered why we had not thought of taking a taxi. By the time we reached Elizabeth's flat and she unlocked her door, my arm was all but paralyzed.

'Dear God, what we do for the love of family,' I muttered, as I struggled to offload the shopping on the kitchen table.

William arrived mid-morning. His first comment as he entered the front door, 'I could smell the lamb from Waterloo Station.'

Sharp as a whistle: 'Not possible,' I laughed, 'with all the obnoxious smells around London.'

Elizabeth, determined to get in her pennyworth, loyal as ever to Londoners, chirped, 'Well, the smog has improved over the years since we no longer heat our homes with coal.'

I was anxious to assist with the cooking because of Elizabeth's fragile health, and offered a helping hand, but she brushed me aside saying, 'Truly, I can manage. But can you make the mint sauce and gravy?'

I was only too happy to oblige!

Having eaten an excellent dinner William and I praised Elizabeth, especially for the thick custard she made to serve over the apple pie. We suggested a well-earned rest with her feet up while William and I cleared the dining table, washed the dishes and put them back on their shelves.

The remainder of our Sunday went all too soon. The living room clock ticked louder as though to warn us it was time for William's departure. The three of us caught the Kensington bus to Waterloo Station, where we said our goodbyes. As he boarded his train I promised to see him and the family in a few day's time, before returning home to Canada. On the journey home by bus, Elizabeth and I chatted about the enjoyable time we had with a caring brother and agreed whenever in his company, we were always sure of a good laugh.

Back in the kitchen, I hurriedly put the kettle on to make tea. Elizabeth was standing at the table with a questioning look on her face as she studied the plate holding the leftover lamb. 'What shall we do with it?' she asked.

'Don't worry,' I said, 'we'll think of some exotic curried dish to use it up.'

LIVING IT UP

The gargantuan meals William cooked for Sunday dinners caused me to pause. I pictured roast beef and Yorkshire puddings over the meat, with piles of vegetables and lashings of thick gravy. The master cook with his long apron over his trousers, fork or spoon in hand, is a sight held dear in the back of my mind. Roasting pork with sage and onion, crackling baked hard, we licked our finger clean without thought of dying of cholesterol on the spot.

Often competing in the skill of culinary art, I must say however hard he tried to come up to scratch with my home-made scones, William never beat me. I boasted the texture of the scones was due to the way hands mixed the butter and flour to create a lightness in the dough by letting it rise and fall in the mixing bowl, before adding the rest of the ingredients. His expression was one of disbelief, and a wicked grin.

Dinners of beef or pork sausages I positively drooled, when he put a plate on the table in front of me. That is until one day I watched him in the kitchen prepare the meal.

With a pound of lard, slapped unceremoniously in a large cooking pan, William topped the mass of fat with a pound of sausages and put them in a hot oven to cook. Meanwhile he prepared the vegetables, cheerfully humming, as he washed and chopped with a large carving knife, without a care in the world. I kept a straight face, as I inhaled the odour from the sausages now seeping from the oven. How much cholesterol would end up in our gall bladders, had me concerned. Then I reasoned to myself, if he puts lots of gravy over them it may help break down the fat. This line of thought did not entirely convince me the gravy would reduce the fat content, as I knew full well it was made from the same fat that came from the sausages. Either way, there was a no win-win answer.

William prided himself in giving a good meal whenever the family visited. A grandson or granddaughter would stand outside the kitchen, watching, sniffing the food coming from the oven. With a long spiked fork he'd take a roasted potato out of the pan with a warning, 'Hot, hot,' as the child gingerly removed it from the fork. One grandson, a boy of nine with dark brown eyes and black hair, often popped in to see his Granddad while I was there, and was a joy to watch. Like a beacon, his face lit up when taking a potato off the fork. Cautiously biting on it in his hand he would stop eating, to give Granddad a big grin. Wiping his fingers on the proffered towel, as he licked his lips, 'Ooh, that was good!'

I was curious to know how William was able to put a tasty dinner on the table without ever using herbs of parsley, rosemary, sage and many others, to bring out the flavour in meat. Cooking simple dishes he enjoyed but if you suggested he prepare a gourmet dish, his nose distinctly turned up. When I asked if he were interested in growing herbs in his garden, the answer was a positive 'No.'

He went through the flow of life doing his own thing, shopping, chatting up the ladies in Asda, in and around Portsmouth and Waterlooville – and with his brown bedroom eyes, suggested they meet him under the old railway clock. Sometimes he dawdled in town, stopping at one of the small cafes for a cup of coffee, or popping into the local for a quickie. His character was contagious to the point it left one wondering how he managed to escape the wrath of husbands whose wives he enjoyed chatting up!

One Sunday afternoon after we trailed around most of the morning in a farmer's field searching for bargains at a boot sale, we came home gasping for a cup of tea, and a sit down. As we waited for the kettle to boil, William took a jam sponge cake out of a tin and laid it on a large plate. He cut a slice of the cake, put it on a tea plate, and handed it to me. I paused, before taking a bite, to ask if he used the same method of weighing the ingredients, before baking. Giving me a sly look and one of his cheeky grins, as though taken off guard, admitted, 'This one came out of a Green's sponge mixture package from Asda.'

'Well,' I said, 'it looks home-baked,' eager to sample the package mixture.

I knew he wasn't one for eating desserts or cakes so was surprised when he said, 'Occasionally, I buy them. It's a time-saver.'

As I munched on another piece of Green's sponge cake, licking the strawberry jam in the centre, I gazed at him without further comment.

Asda is a sprawling supermarket in Waterlooville selling all and sundry, including bedding, clothing items and other household necessities as well as dairy products, meats, fruits and vegetables. Their cold-cut counter is virgin white clean, with trays holding a variety of meats and pies that whet the appetite the minute one approaches. I was never however impressed with their donuts, compared to North American style, which puts them to shame. Not only were they too sweet but the fat used to make them seemed overkill, and the price much too high.

Getting to the supermarket was easy enough, as we went by taxi. William loved shopping at Asda where he could "chivvy" up the ladies.

After shopping, customers waiting for taxis were left standing in line outside the supermarket an appreciable length of time, to return home. This waiting peeved William no end. He hated having to stand around, particularly when it drizzled rain. The driver bore the full brunt of his customer's frustration as he pulled up the taxi in front of us, and we climbed in. Without warning, William would suddenly chat up a storm to the poor driver who hadn't a clue what his passenger's anger was all about, in the first place. Gradually, as William relaxed in the seat next to the driver, his mind tuned into his favourite sport, horse-racing.

He rambled non-stop about the horses running that day at a certain race course.

Nudging the driver, he'd say. 'If you're a betting man put a few quid on a non favourite, to win.' The driver's expression was one of disbelief. For seconds, he averted his eyes off the road, cautiously turning to look at his passenger, and wondered if this was the same angry man he had picked up outside Asda who now sat laughing beside him, as though his ribs would burst.

Curiosity knows no bounds. I was itching to know how he made Madeira cakes and asked myself if I wasn't touching on another baking mystery, so decided to wait until he was more forthcoming as to the method he used. I never did get the opportunity to watch. He did however give me his recipe, which I use to this day.

Friday was the one day of the week he neither baked or cooked, or ate meat. It was a ritual going back to religious beginnings, when only fish was allowed to be eaten. When I was visiting, it was left up to me to trot to the local fish and chip shop round the corner from where William lived, and buy Friday's dinner. I must confess the fish, if not the chips, was delicious.

Our usual trips to the sandy shores of Dorset where we stayed either at the Crown Hotel (or the King's Head depended on the time of booking and available space), I looked forward to. Once positive of my flight plans, and place of arrival, William would go ahead and book accommodation in one of the hotels. We liked the Crown for its friendliness. The cuisine was excellent. Extra pounds of weight gained through eating full English breakfast, lunch and dinner, was something I was eager to offload soon as I arrived back in Canada. Our time at the Crown was never long enough. It went in a flash!

We left Weymouth by taxi, passing through familiar villages and farmland. Many large estates nestled in acres of prime land, where cattle were seen to graze. Thorough-bred horses rested leisurely in stalls after a hunt or race, and appeared content as they listened to the wild birds that fed in the fields, notably the testy magpies strutting over smaller birds. Why the magpie never failed to catch my attention on every visit to and from Dorset, caused me to ponder.

As our taxi drew up to the front door of William's home, my brother had one thought in mind. To plan his next fruit cake.

THE BARE TRUTH

In 2005, William told me that after a recent visit to his eye specialist it was confirmed his right eye showed a partial loss of sight and a condition known as macular degenerative, as the cause. Not only was he devastated when hearing this news, but family members worried because it was an added concern on top of his other health problems.

William would not talk about the operations he had undergone in the Navy until one day I questioned his pain level on the right side of his body. His face was distorted in agony. Lifting up his shirt he showed me the long scars that circled from the rib cage across to his lower back, and pointed to the area where one of his kidneys had been removed. I was so shocked at this evidence of patchwork. It left me gasping!

'My God,' I cried. 'It's brutal they could do this to you.'

The vision of my brother under the Naval surgeon's knife, did not bear thinking about. How the system worked in the armed services in time of war when a man's life is at risk, the general public would have little knowledge of procedure. Gazing at the scars I imagined the scene on the operating table, as it unfolded.

William took my outburst of concern with remarkable calm. 'It's done and over with.' Adding, 'the operations probably saved my life, so I cope as best I can.'

I paused as I digested his off-handed remark, thinking it prudent not to aggravate him with the question: 'How do you know?' and remained silent.

To lighten our moods, with my hand on his right shoulder, I rambled on about his skill with the sewing needle and the art of crocheting he learned during his convalescent days in the hospital. I never did know the name of the hospital he was in but at a guess feel sure it would be at a British Naval Port either in Malta or Gibraltar; these being the two ports where his ship regularly docked.

In our many discussions about his life aboard ships I sensed that while his past health problems were not over yet, this latest scourge with his right eye grieved him more than the loss of a kidney. Which, of course, was bad enough! But in his thinking, he would rather lose a limb than an eye, seemed to sum up his usual philosophy.

What I found even more remarkable about his character was that when we spoke over the phone every Sunday for one hour, he never mentioned the problem with his right eye when I inquired how he was keeping. It wasn't until my next visit to him, he casually mentioned it.

We greeted each other at Heathrow Airport, and took a taxi to Hampshire. Once seated, we were on our way from London to Waterlooville, travelling through familiar farmlands, and seeing herds of cows pasturing or resting in the fields. On every visit to Hampshire I never tired of looking down from my seat inside the aircraft at the patchwork quilt of the English countryside, as the plane gently approached the airstrip ahead.

Chatting about all and sundry on our journey to Hampshire, William appeared reluctant to bring up the subject of his eye problem. I wanted to hear the full details about his eye and if there was some kind of treatment available to cure or keep it from deteriorating further, but decided to let the matter rest while I sat listening to his latest family news. His arm slipped through mine as though to say, 'All's well.'

Once home and we settled down in the living room with cups of tea in our hands, munching on Peak Frean biscuits, I was agog for news but knew I would have to wait until the teacups were washed and put back in the kitchen cupboard. His rigid routine of timing and doing everything correctly by the book, I feel, stemmed from his early training in the Navy. I have never known a man to be so particular in keeping to a regular pattern of routine, of how things should be done.

His right eye had deteriorated to the point he was no longer able to see without the use of a large magnifying glass. One early morning, I watched him crouched over the dining table with the glass in front of him. He shifted it from the top to the bottom of the Daily Mail newspaper column to see which horses were running in that day's races. Not being able to see the names of the horses running, or the lines on the betting slip, he became agitated.

I whispered in his ear, 'Can I help?'

Raising up his head he looked at me and said, 'Would you?' with a sad look on his face as though he were about to die.

Trying to perk him up, thinking nothing ventured, nothing gained, 'Of course, I'll help,' I replied, light-heartedly.

Sitting at the dining room table, pen poised, we buried our heads over the newspaper and studied the form of each horse running at a number of race courses. Giving considerable thought to possible winners and selecting several, he showed me how to make out the betting slip. I had hardly put pen to paper, with instructions on how much money to put on each horse, when I realized he was ahead of me with the calculations on each bet, as I scratched furiously away to put down the name of the right horse and the correct number on the betting slip.

The slip completed, I wondered what on Earth I had let myself in for.

With a casual complacency I slid on my seat in the taxi, the money in my purse, and the betting slip tucked safely in my coat pocket. When the driver pulled up outside the betting shop, I paid his fare. I stood looking at the shop door painted a sickly green and wondered what element of surprise faced me, as I gently opened it. Cautiously entering the sanctuary of a smoke-filled room it took a second or two to get my bearing to breathe through a thick haze of blue fumes, swirling like belly dancers up to the ceiling, reminiscent of past London pea fogs. The gamblers, all men, were facing the wide inside walls holding large screens of the horses currently running, hoping they had picked a winner. The minute I entered their domain, all chatter stopped. All eyes were upon me.

Giving a weak smile I sauntered up to the counter where a clerk, showing a cleavage that would be the pride of every actress young and old, took the betting slip from me.

'Four pounds, ducks!'

I was appalled she would address a client, albeit, one acting on behalf of a brother, in this manner. She surprised me further by asking if I'd like a cup of coffee. As this scenario played out, all the men stopped looking at the screens as I passed the betting money over the counter and picked up the slips. A few gave cheeky grins. I thanked her, and declined the coffee.

As time went by, learning the skill of filling out a betting slip was more of a surprise to me than William, as I caught on to it remarkably well. After breakfast, we lingered over the dining table and studied the daily newspapers, debating on which horse we thought might be a possible winner. I was becoming as addicted to the races of the day as my brother, and enthused when he agreed on a horse I had picked to win. Seldom did he chose a favourite running with poor odds.

'Think of the cash I would lose if my choice of a runner didn't get to the winning post,' was a comment I heard often.

Knowing many of his cronies in the betting shop were compulsive gamblers who not only ran up heavy debts, some losing the shirts off their backs, this was one avenue William was determined would never be on his agenda. Although accepted by his gambling cronies at the betting shop it became abundantly clear one or two of them did not appreciate his style of gambling and showed their annoyance with his repeated wins, betting twenty pence on each horse. How, they wondered, could he win so much, paying out so little. He was not about to give away secrets.

My trips to the betting shop continued throughout my stay in Hampshire. As time passed, the gamblers stopped to chat, puffing on cigarettes that blew smoke in my face and on my clothes. I could but endure, knowing William's bet was placed as I headed silently out of the door.

Not only did we place bets on the horses, but also on the annual rowing regatta held at Henley-on-Thames, SE Oxfordshire and 7 miles NNE of Reading, Berkshire. Reading's history dates from 871, when it was occupied by the Danes. The Benedictine Abbey was founded 1121 by Henry I, who is buried here. Oscar Wilde wrote his *Ballad of Reading Gaol* while imprisoned in this town.

The annual rowing regatta began in 1839. This event draws large crowds far and wide from across the country and abroad to watch the rowers from Oxford and Cambridge universities, compete. Along the tow path beside the river, university students meander as though to give visitors a chance to see them conspicuously, wearing straw boaters on their heads, and striped blazers, as they watched the race in earnest, hoping their team would win. Without studying the skills of either team, my choice to win was Oxford, wearing dark blue. William, on the other hand, chose Cambridge, light blue.

I picked Oxford because of a nostalgic connection. On September 2,1945, Japan surrendered and was under Allied military occupation. General Douglas MacArthur was the Supreme Commander. On that day, called "VJ Day", my husband and I were driving in a red MG sports car, heading to Monmouthshire, South Wales. We stopped in Oxford for a meal at our regular restaurant, before continuing our journey towards the Bristol Channel. As we reached the city, the noise was deafening. Unbeknown to us, the people were celebrating victory of Japan's surrender. They were dancing in the streets in large circles, singing, drinking from bottles, throwing caution to the wind, come high or low, should the local police stop the excitement of activities. No one cared. The atmosphere was of a hurricane erupting through the city, out of control. The celebration of victory went on till the early hours of the morning. We stayed overnight in Oxford, not to miss the fun!

Next morning, we left the city and heading toward open country, spotted many hares and rabbits on the roadside dying of myxomatosis, a disease introduced by the government to stop them from over-breeding. This action was taken because the farmers bitterly complained the rabbits and hares were swarming their lands, and eating acres of good crops. Later, it was learned this form of rabbit control came initially from Australian agricultural authorities who, for years, were dealing with similar problems. It was to take decades before the rabbit population recovered from this contagious and deadly virus disease.

Despite the fact many people saw fit to bet on a royal birth, prince or princess, this one event did not appeal sufficiently enough to William for him to place a bet. Hill's, the renowned bookie, coffers would not swell with his money. Form of study is what absorbed William's interest in horses, and it remained with him regardless of losing the sight in one eye, later in his life, to continue with a pleasure he found intriguing, and a way to dabble in pennies. It was not the monetary value, so much, as the joy of hood-winking the bookies whenever the chance presented itself.

OTHER HIDDEN TALENTS

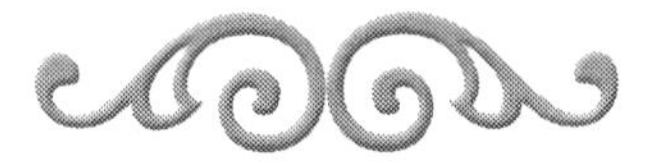

Life in the Royal Navy is known to be an excellent starting off point for young men and women, as it teaches them survival skills in wartime and in peace. At best, most people go through life dealing with the pros and cons of any situation in the hope their choices will direct them to a life of fulfilment. Often choosing one of the armed services was a route to achieve this goal.

The armed forces develop unknown character in those who choose or are compelled through hostilities to adorn the King's uniform inasmuch as when a soldier, sailor or airman comes to the fore and is ill-equipped either through lack of education or living a home life which does not complement untapped skills, it can be amazing what extensive training can do to bring out untapped potential. What develops throughout his service exposes his character, and determines what path lies ahead.

In William's case, as a teenager, he was expected to undertake many chores which he sometimes only did begrudgingly. However, when he voluntarily joined the Royal Navy he never sniffed at any opportunity coming his way if he thought it enhanced a better chance for himself and his family, once he returned to civilian life.

His on-going talents were many. Up at the crack of dawn before the early birds of song chirped their greeting to a sunny morning, William stood at the ironing board in the dining room pressing out each crease on sleeves and tails of shirts that hung on hooks over the kitchen door. He appeared to enjoy this first task of the day and kept to a regular routine of washing, ironing and airing clothes on tall wooden slats held on a clothes horse, on a weekly basis. As he went about his business, these chores held him deep in concentration. I often wondered if his life with Violet flowed through his head as he held the steaming iron firmly in his hand, moving it back and forth over the ironing board, his body language relaxed and content.

Despite the difference in personalities, the marriage was good. Violet, was a gentle person. William was a flamboyant character who wanted to make the world laugh at every turn. How these two people immersed their individuality to blend with one another caused me to think that indeed life is full of surprises. The adage, "one of a kind", says it all!

Music was an endless passion to William and his two sisters. To Elizabeth and I, there was no music preferable to the classics. William's choice of music came from New York and the London shows. The Beatles he enjoyed. Their music however did nothing to arouse the emotions of his sisters. I must confess my tolerance of them was short and sweet. Listening to the classics and the strains of the violin, my soul left my body as it floated upward to a heavenly sky in a state of euphoria. After an evening's concert either at the Albert Hall or the Festival Hall in London, the following morning the reality of life stared me in the face, as I gently landed back to Earth.

Living at Petts Wood, Kent in the early 1960s, Elizabeth and I met in London to go to one of the many seasonal concerts held at the Albert Hall where conductors of fame, Adrian Bolt, Thomas Beecham and Malcom Sargeant, performed. All three masters received knighthoods. Sir Malcolm Sargeant, one of the best known modern British conductors, succeeded Sir Adrian Bolt as permanent conductor of the B.B.C. Symphony Orchestra 1950-1957. In later years, he lost his eyesight. These concerts held in the 1950s and '60s were extremely popular with music-lovers of all ages, and unless one booked well in advance or bought seasonal tickets, it was difficult to get a seat.

It was never a problem for Elizabeth to get to the concert, as the buses from her home in Kensington stopped outside the hall. On the other hand, my journey entailed catching a train from PettsWood railway station to Waterloo, London, then either taxi-ing or taking the bus to the hall where she would be waiting at the entrance to greet me. When the concert finished we followed the crowd and gradually made our way outside, chatting non-stop about the evening's performance while waiting to catch our bus to Kensington, all the while declaring we were madly in love as ever with our conductor, especially if it was Sir Malcom Sargeant.

What secrets lie in the strings of a violin that cause the sensitive ear to listen in a state of utter bliss and give the feeling of floating on a moon-beam, across a sky of glittering stars?

On my return journey home to Petts Wood, my head in a cloud, I would suddenly be alerted back to reality as the train puffed its way to a stop at my station, for me to get off. I walked home in a musical dream until I put the house key in its lock, and came back down, once more, to Earth.

William certainly did not possess a voice for singing, but when he sang he was happy as a lark, even though I often "ribbed" him about his lack of musical skill. His response to my teasing, was a wide grin, then a rendition of his favourite tune, *"Tell Laura I Love Her"*. Secretly, I wondered if he was harbouring a new-found lady friend, he had yet to introduce to me. After listening to the same song, finally, I piped up, 'Why don't you sing: "Tell Darlene I Love Her"?'

'You're taking the Micky,' he grinned, his brown eyes laughing at me.

Giving me a look second to none, I had the distinct feeling he was trying to tell me how much he missed Darlene and wished her back. Sadly we both knew, there was no turning point. Darlene had made it abundantly clear she would not put up with the nasty treatment from his family that splintered their marriage like shard glass, and caused the break-up. I had the greatest admiration for my sister-in-law. She was not a person who believed in mincing her words. Down to Earth, she took life for what it had to offer with a hearty, throaty laugh. Beneath the facade however when speaking over the phone, her voice portrayed a note of deep sadness.

Gardening, we both enjoyed with a passion. Many times in William's garden at Crookhorn, I praised him on the quality of the tomatoes grown in the greenhouse, along the south wall. An ideal location, it provided light, warmth and sunshine to grow large red tomatoes. Unfortunately, he never enjoyed the fruits of his labour, due to a hernia problem. If I suggested having one for lunch, it pleased him no end. He would go to the greenhouse, pluck the ripest off the vine, wash, slice it and put it on a salad plate for me. Overripe tomatoes were given to his favourite neighbours who were fully aware his cheeky suggestions to meet him under the old railway clock at Portsmouth proved as blunt as an old sewing-needle but they went along with his chivvying, hoping to get more.

If a leaf fell off an African Violet plant it was held in high esteem, as though William was holding a bar of gold in his hand. He carefully lifted the centre of the stem he put in a small glass vase half-filled with water, and stood it on the living room window ledge until spidery roots began to appear. The ledge also held a variety of violets: pink, white and mauve in colourful ceramic pots, facing the light. The profusion of shades always caught the eye.

One day, casually strolling through the town of Waterlooville I spotted the one and only fruiterer who sold not only fruit and vegetables but also a sparse assortment of plants, looking in dire need of tender loving care. Picking up a tiny plastic pot holding a pink African Violet, I took it to where a man was standing behind the counter, and handed him coins to the price shown on the pot. He did not offer to put my purchase in a plastic bag so I put the pot gently in my handbag, hoping it would survive by the time I reached home.

Arriving back late afternoon, I buzzed the front door intercom of the apartment building where William lived, so I could get in. I removed my overcoat then with the utmost care, took the tiny pot out of my handbag. Holding my precious gift, I handed it to him. Looking at it, he gave me a wide grin.

'Guess, you're not going to tell me how much you paid for it?'

'Well,' I said. 'One isn't supposed to question the price of a gift, is one? But since you're so anxious to know, I'll tell you. It was three pounds.'

In the snap of an eyelid: 'I know the blighter you bought it from. Talk about daylight robbery.'

I let him continue with his spiel, smiled at him, said, 'Hope you like it.'

At his Crookhorn property he grew several rows of runner beans entwined on tall spindly sticks that stood in a wide bed of horse manure soil, supported by a deep wooden frame. By the time these were ready for picking and eating, I had returned home to Canada.

My mother-in-law, Septre May Harris, born 1902 in Mid Glamorgan, South Wales, was of medium height. She washed her tawny colour hair in mountain water, to give it a brilliant shine. Her nose was small and straight. Her pale blue eyes were sharp as a razor. Notorious for keeping a close watch on her neighbours whose daily attire included large hair rollers that covered their heads, she listened in earnest when they gathered on their doorsteps to indulge in daily gossip. Known as Sep, she married George Frederick Whitehead, born 1897 in Eckington, Derbyshire, in Pontpridd, Glamorgan 1921. Like her brother and sisters, she was extremely good-looking. Her siblings possessed the same high-strung character, which appeared to stem direct from their father, William Harris, born 1873 in Bedwellty/Argoed, Monmouthshire.

Whenever I met him, his blue eyes seemed to bore into the depth of my soul. He would simply look at me without saying a word. Ever more frightening, the permanent scowl on his face caused his bushy eyebrows to furrow to a deep crease over his eyes, giving the impression he was about to go into one of his rambunctious moods. There was never any question in my mind who was master of his household. On my visits to Wales I cannot remember at any time having a conversation with him. Even if it were remotely possible, where would I begin?

Between the experienced and the inexperienced I constantly goaded myself, would I be ready, on the day of judgement. Then questioned, was I able to judge this reticent relative in my capacity as the young wife of his grandson, or would he be brutal in his judgement simply because his grandson had not married a Welsh girl?

Upon reflection, he was a man whose strongest urge was the protection of his family, albeit, now long grown and married. Although it took me some time to evaluate where he came from, I found myself silently agreeing with him on discussions inside and outside the home. After a hard day working in the mines and eating a hearty supper, with his pipe in hand and smoking some dreadful-smelling tobacco, his feet upon a low stool near the fireplace, he relaxed in complacent silence. Looking at the scene before me I was touched by the affection of this close-knit group who through the rites of marriage, were now family to me.

Like my brother William, Grandfather Harris loved the horses and never a Saturday passed when miner and doctor were seen driving from the miner's house to the race meet. Where this meet took place, no one knew.

Sep, my mother-in-law, was skilful in processing runner beans, as well as other home-grown produce. At work in the kitchen, a serious expression on her face, in full concentration on the task at hand, she washed and strung the beans. Using a potato peeler she scored down each side of the bean to remove the stringy part, topped and tailed both ends, or scraped with a paring knife any other part of the bean that looked remotely inedible. The runners were then sliced vertically with a sharp knife and put in a large bowl. They were then ladled into a big earthenware jar between layers of salt, ready for winter's table when vegetables were either in short supply, or too costly to buy. When cooked, the beans tasted as though they had just been picked from the garden.

Sep's skill at stretching a pound sterling to unknown quantities, left me in awe. Buying a three-pennyworth of stewing steak, a portion of the meat was served with vegetables, or turned into a meat pie. With luck, any leftover scraps of steak were made into rissoles. Nothing was wasted, not even the fat off the meat, grudgingly spared to make suet puddings.

Apple pie made on a dinner plate, was baked to perfection in the side oven of an old black range. Years later, I was horrified to learn the plates used to make the pies were antique plates which belonged to her family for generations. The fine porcelain with delicate designs on the plates never cracked during the baking.

Compared to the profusion of flowers in William's garden beds, vegetables consisted of tomatoes, runner beans and a marrow piled high on top of a mound of stinky manure in the corner of his garden. The smell was enough to put the resident hedgehog off its trail as it nosed its way from one end of the garden to the next, in the hope of a meal.

One of William's neighbours was audacious enough to ask, 'what's that smell coming from your garden?' Explaining to her the dung was good manure for growing marrows, she put her nose in the air and before slamming shut her back door, yelled, 'Should have had Council's permission to use that horrible stuff!'

I said to William, 'Aren't you afraid she might jump the fence one night and steal the marrow?'

'No, never,' was his remark. 'She'd tear her one and only fleecy nightgown, if she did.'

A clucking sound came from the back of his throat, his brown eyes laughing.

His one talent which never came to fruition was to write a book. When William told me this was his dream I tried not to linger doubts in my head but wondered when put to the test, if he was serious. I confess to being somewhat taken aback when he told me the title of the book. The words flew out of his mouth: *"The Virgin Matelot."*

I had visions of sailors wearing angelic wings. 'You must be joking,' I laughed.

'One in every port,' he grinned, tapping one finger to the side of his nose. 'There was a book published called *"The Virgin Soldier"*. Ever heard of it?'

'Virgins, in the armed forces,' I said, unable to control my mirth. 'Other sexual encounters no doubt, but virgins, ooh!, think not!'

I dropped the subject like a thunderbolt!

CLOCKS AND WATCHES

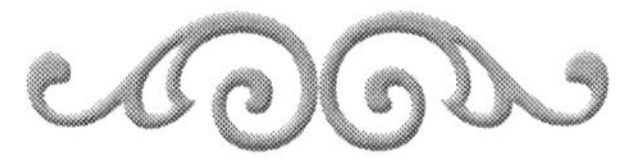

There was not a clock or watch needing repair, William could not fix. A large white cloth was placed on the dining table, to avoid damage to the oak wood when he used pointed tweezers to pick up coiled springs, time hands and rounds of perspex glass that covered the face of clocks and broken watches. Large or small, they were dismantled and all parts put in a square metal tin. With a magnifying glass on the tip of his nose, a pair of tweezers in one hand, operation commenced at a serious pace. Family or foe were not allowed to disturb him while he worked.

Grandfather clocks were a challenge. One day, quietly sitting in a chair by the side of William, I watched as he gently twisted a tiny knob at the back of a grandfather clock held in a mahogany cabinet, and removed the mechanism from inside. It left me wondering how he would put all parts back to their original condition with the big and small hands working, to make the clock tick and chime again. It never concerned William. All the parts for repairs he kept in a tin box holding a variety of springs some old, some new. Either through trial and error or pure luck, he was able to find the ones that worked. More often than not, the used parts of old clocks and watches fitted perfectly to the one he had on hand, to repair. Since this was a work of love to his family and friends, he never asked for payment of service when clocks of all shapes and sizes were left at his door.

To add to this pleasurable hobby, not having to purchase new parts for repairs made the task of bringing the melodious ticking of a clock and chimes back to life, even more worthy of time spent.

Many moons ago, when I lived in England, I once asked him to repair a lady's old wristwatch and confess to thinking, 'He'll never get this one to go.'

But, I erred in my judgement about his perseverance to deal with something so antiquated. One of the tiny hands had broken off and I was sure he had no replacement in his tin box. Neither, I assumed, would he find one in a jeweller's shop due to its age.

A few weeks later we met in a Surrey tea shop and over a cup of tea, he took a case out of his coat pocket and placed it in front of me on the table. I opened the lid of the case and found the antiquated wristwatch, picked it up, and put it to my ear. A pleasant tick, ticking sound was heard, as the tiny hand moved with the grace of a ballerina, its glass face shone like a new moon.

Putting the watch back in its case I asked my brother, 'Where did you find the new hand?'

'Well, luck really! This little old watchmaker whom I've known for years, now retired from the business and lives in the next town, I took the off-chance in popping in to see him. When he opened his front door to me and saw who it was, he invited me in. I explained what I was looking for, and asked if he could help. Wearing carpet slippers he shuffled along the hallway and went to a small cupboard under the stairwell, and pulled out a black box.'

'Think this might do the trick,' he said, as he took the cover off the box and placed its contents on the kitchen table.

As the two men sorted through a conglomerate of mechanical pieces, they chose several parts plus a small hand, which might fit. The old watchmaker was happy to give whatever William needed, at no cost.

After listening to this visit with an old friend I said, 'No doubt you came home all smiles with your treasures.'

'Well, the best part of my visit was that the piece he gave me fits like a new glove, as though made for the wristwatch.'

Occasionally, when William offered to repair a friend's grandfather clock and it was too difficult to transport, due to its size and weight, he taxied to the house and did the repairs there. He never replaced the old parts with the new parts until he had thoroughly cleaned the inside and outside panels of the wood cabinet. Seeing a smile on his friend's face as he listened to his prized clock or watch ticking, William beamed with satisfaction of a job well done.

He took a keen interest in marine chronometers, having served over a period of 26 years in His Majesty's Royal Navy. A chronometer is an instrument that measures time with exactness, used to determine the longitude at sea by the difference between its time and solar time. The National Maritime Museum at Greenwich, London has individual chronometers recorded, as well as a collection of marine chronometers dating back to the early 1800s.

Noted among famous English names, Asprey, Dent, Hatton, Russells and Losada connected with chronometers, James McCabe's two-day chronometer, the dial 8.5 cm, the case fitted with a convex glass, circa 1827, was first supplied to *HMS Meda* at Greenwich 1828, but he was not a maker. The marine chronometers were made for these merchants with their names engraved on the dials. They acted as retailers.

One of Dent's chronometers was used on *Her Majesty's Ship Beagle*, the renowned ship which in the 1830s took Charles Darwin on his famous voyage. His formulated theory on evolution, *"The Origin of the Species"*, was published in 1859.

By 1840-1880, eight-day chronometers were manufactured. Russell's of Liverpool, maker to the Japanese government, made dials with gold hands. The chronometer had a steel helical (wire or thread wound in a single layer round a cylinder, a spiral) balance spring and a set of three metal rings so pivoted one within the other it maintains an object supported by it, such as a ship's compass, in a mahogany box.

Thomas Mercer of St. Alban's, near London, still producing mechanical marine chronometers, showing the five stages of a chronometer balance and a number of compensated balance variations, are the only firm to do so in the world today

On William's seventieth birthday I gave him a much-wanted gold fob watch, with his initials inscribed. I sensed this request was to keep him in tune with his swaggering, carefree nature.

Fob watches are held by a gold chain with a clip at one end, and attached to a gentleman's waistcoat, to avoid it slipping out. If the gentleman is left-handed, the fob is put in the right-hand pocket and the gold chain clipped to his left pocket. If he was a right-handed person, the fob is reversed.

Going back to the early 1700s and 1800s, the fob or watch pocket was formerly in the waistband of breeches. Today, few men are seen with gentlemen's waistcoats or wearing breeches, unless horse-riding.

A miniature grandfather clock, given to me as a wedding gift by my Welsh and Derbyshire in-laws, is covered in a cloth and sits on the top shelf in my bedroom closet. Silent. It has not chimed or ticked in years, and awaits the hand of Providence to bring it alive.

William calls down from above, 'Don't worry, it will tick again, one day.'

STAMP COLLECTOR

His Royal Mail stamp collection began in 1946, with a number of special issues commemorating events as far back to 1642.

It was not until I emigrated to Canada the first time in 1956, that I became aware of this hobby. (With my family, we boarded a ship from Southampton docks in England to the shores of Wolfe's Cove, Quebec. The ship transported not only English migrants to a chosen country, but also hundreds of Hungarian refugees fleeing from the revolution.)

When hearing from William that his eldest son Daniel was also a stamp collector, I became interested in collecting and sharing with them stamps not only from England, but throughout the world.

Over many decades, William sent first issue English stamps bought either at the local post office or through The Royal Mint. As his interest in stamps widened, we arranged to exchange these with Canadian issues. This kept both of our collections updated with the flow of new issues between the two countries. When the mail arrived my curiosity increased as to which stamp, commemorating a special event, would be added to my collection. Other than news from the radio or the television, until I opened the special Royal Mail envelope with the commemorative stamps inside, I had no idea what it was he had mailed. My brother was of a nature that the more surprises one had in life, the more the world ticked like the proverbial grandfather clocks and wristwatches he diligently repaired.

During one of his visits to Canada I showed him my world collection, including commemorative stamps of Terry Fox on his Marathon of Hope run, each worth 30 cents. In April 1980, a remarkable one-legged runner from British Columbia named Terry Fox set off across Canada on a journey known as the Marathon of Hope, to raise money for cancer research. He died before completing the distance but succeeded in raising $21 million by year's end. He was awarded the Lou Marsh Trophy as Canada's Athlete of the Year.

William's collection included many of considerable interest today:

The 1642–1951 issue of The Civil War fought between the forces of King and Parliament. The stamps show Pikeman, Drummer, Musketeer and Standard Bearer.

1754–2004 first issue featuring Sir Rowland Hill, a member of The Royal Society for the encouragement of Arts, Manufacturers and Commerce, who was awarded the first RSA Albert Medal in 1804 for his postal reforms and the introduction of the Penny Post.

1805–2005, first issue commemorating the Battle of Trafalgar.

1840–1928, this 20-pence stamp was issued to celebrate the one hundred and fiftieth anniversary of Thomas Hardy, one of Britain's respected writers. Born in the Dorset hamlet of Higher Bockhampton in 1840, he was the son of a stonemason.

1840–1990, this miniature sheet contains one of the stamps featuring the famous portrait head of H.M. Queen Victoria to mark the one hundred and fiftieth anniversary of the Penny Black.

1840–1990, Kew Gardens, formerly a private royal garden. Since 1840 it became a national institution. It borders the River Thames in the western outskirts of London. The stamps portray the Pagoda with a cedar tree.

1854–56, The Crimean War stamps denote the infamous Charge of the Light Brigade.

1916–2006, Lest We Forget the Battle of the Somme, July through November 1916. The poem *"In Flanders Fields"* was written by John McCrae, a surgeon to the First Canadian Field Artillery.

1944, the Stamp Card Series of D-Day. Advancing from Ouistreham. Ground crew reloading RAF Bostons. Commandos Landing on Gold Beach. Coastal Bombardment by *"HMS Warspite"*. Infantry regrouping on Sword Beach.

1980 series on Music, portraying four British Conductors – Sir Henry Wood, Sir Malcolm Sargeant, Sir John Barbirolli and Sir Thomas Beecham.

William and I continued to exchange collector's stamps up to the year 2005, when life was beginning to take its toll on his health. We had spoken many times of his wish that I would inherit his collection. When I eventually received four of the six volumes he possessed, I was somewhat taken aback to find the Royal Mail Presentation Pack containing the Canadian stamps I had sent him over the years, were not included. I wonder about family interference in the estate. Going back to the 1940s, the collections in his six volumes had been valued at 15,000 pounds sterling.

MEMORABLE JOURNEYS

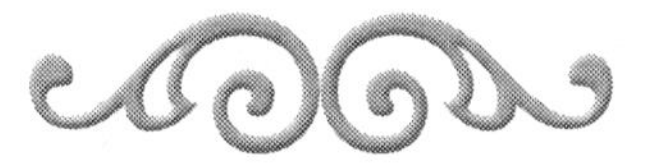

Trips from Portsmouth by ferry took several hours to reach the Channel Islands of Jersey and Guernsey. At any time of the year English people jaunted back and forth in sleek ferries, well-furnished and well-stocked with a variety of saleable merchandise, including liquor, which when bought on the ferry or on one of the islands, was tax-free.

It took me by surprise on one such trip to see happy travellers returning home with cartloads of wine and beer and sail through customs when the ferry docked at Portsmouth, without an official so much as checking for contraband.

Guernsey is the closest of the two islands from Portsmouth. Its Chamber of Commerce's colourful magazine boasts about a mild climate, making it a popular holiday resort. Like Jersey, Guernsey is known for its breed of cattle. Fertile soil and adequate rainfalls and the nearness to markets have made the growing of vegetables, flowers and fruits a viable industry. Much of the island's produce is shipped to Covent Garden market in London where it is distributed to various towns in different parts of the country.

There is however a stark different between these islands. Upon reaching St. Helier where the ferry docks, leaving the quayside to reach the town, the traveller finds it necessary to walk up a steep hill to get to the shops. For some, it is a monumental task. Having reached the town, with barely enough minutes to shop before the ferry leaves to return to Portsmouth, it is a case of whether to dash thither here, there and quickly make purchases, often inadvertently, to descend the grade and arrive back at the quayside in breathless time to catch the last ferry of the day.

Farmers on the islands tell many wartime stories when in 1940, they were invaded by the enemy. All livestock, pigs, cows, chickens and sheep were diligently recorded on a daily roster on each farm and were thoroughly checked over by an officer of the regime to ensure food was available to feed their soldiers. However, to survive, the farmers were more wily than their arch enemy. Many dug deep holes in fields during the hours of darkness, with a neighbouring friend watching alertly for their foes, and stashed away fruit and vegetables in wooden barrels as a precaution to further reductions in civilian rations.

Trying to hide a hog or two was a difficult task as the daily roster could not, without risk of life, show reductions of livestock unless an animal suffered a malaise and was authorized to be shot, burned, or as might have been the case, eaten by several farmers' families. The Germans were, to say the least, hardly stupid when a farmer was brought to count why one of his livestock was missing. The reason required substantial verification, or orders given to shoot, if diseased. The Germans had no intention to risk eating contaminated meat. One could but guess the carcass of animals was dissected and split up between different families who ate the meat knowing the tricks used to make an animal look sick, when actually it was in the best of health, quite safe to eat. How long could this trick prevail before the enemy realized it was being hook-winked by the farmers, who enjoyed the spoils with unadulterated pleasure, was anyone's guess.

Jersey is much in tune to the needs of tourists. William and I found the walk from Saint Peter Port quayside much kinder on the limbs, primarily due to being a short distance to the town. Upon arrival at the Port one notices the extreme cleanliness of the area, as well as the bus station nearby. A German underground hospital built during hostilities, now preserved as a war museum, did not absorb our interest.

'We don't need to be reminded of the useless killing of thousands during the war,' William commented, as we boarded a bus to revisit the pearl factory.

Once inside the factory we saw many new designs of jewellery displayed on polished wood shelves, and studied them with interest. Pristine pearls brilliantly exhibited on red and blue velvet cushions held on shelves in glass cases, also on top of the glass counter, caught our eye. I picked up a red velvet case and looked at the three strands of pearls that stretched from the top of the case to the end of the case. Temptation to buy was uppermost in my head. Then I questioned myself, 'What would I do with two sets of pearl necklaces?' William had already bought me two strands of pearls in a shell-shaped case the year before, with matching earrings.

I moved along the centre of the glass counter, with the eyes of the shop assistant upon me as if waiting to pounce for a possible sale. A brooch of a butterfly with wings the colours of a rainbow and one pearl in the centre of its body, caught my attention. An exquisite piece. Sensing my interest, William took the brooch from my hand and placed it on the counter where the young shop assistant now stood smiling, when he said, 'We'll take it.' As she punched the price of the brooch in the cash machine and handed him his change, she flashed a wide smile, saying, 'I will gift-wrap it for you, sir.'

Outside the pearl factory, I thanked William for his gift, and with a wave of his hand he brushed it aside. 'Now you have another memory to take home with you, how about lunch?'

The islands boast good restaurants, serving excellent meals of local meat, fruits and vegetables. Creamy desserts made from the milk of Jersey cows, dared one to ask for a second helping.

On the corner of every street in Guernsey and Jersey, models of different breeds of cows stand tall as live animals, and cause visitors to stop and look. Lifelike, one imagines the model cows walking off the street corner on to the road. The inhabitants on the islands are friendly people, and when war came to their farms it was with imaginative resources and ingenuity they were able to survive.

Sark, the smallest of the three islands, is seven miles east of Guernsey; three and a half mile long, two miles wide. Its local government is based on survival of the feudal system. Recorded population of six hundred, it may have risen slightly over the years; however the island is protected by strict regulations that all newcomers are endowed in sufficient wealth, preferably millionaires, before being allowed to buy land and settle on the island. Due to the width and breadth of Sark one is able to cycle in the narrow lanes from the top of the island to the end of the island, within minutes.

In 2001, we took the ferry from Portsmouth to Bilbao in Northern Spain. To reach Bilbao, it was necessary to go through the Bay of Biscay. Located in the Celtic Sea, a gulf of the North East Atlantic Ocean is called Bay of Biscay. The average depth of the bay is 1745 metres and the maximum depth is 2790 metres. Merchant vessels have reported losing direction in Biscay storms. The German U-boats ruled the Bay and many British and American ships were sunk that entered her waters. Countless ships were wrecked as a result of gruesome weather. The seas, rough and unrelenting with ferociously high winds and swells, cause ships to roll drunkenly with each sicken thud against her side, to its command.

In the 19th century, Spain was ravaged by civil wars, military coups and dictatorships. The Popular Front won a victory in the 1936 elections, which precipitated the great civil war of 1936-39. Under the leadership of General Francisco Franco, the insurgents faced the Loyalist forces which were supported by the nationalists in Catalonia and the Basque Provinces.

We docked at Bilbao round noon, in bright sunny weather. Guided by our driver we stepped into a luxury coach and when all passengers were counted and seated, he drove from the docks along the highway. As we neared the city, colourful shrubs and hanging flower baskets were seen along the boulevards. Against a clear blue sky, the spirals of its Gothic churches stood tall, and glistened in the sunlight. Our coach driver, also our tour guide, was anxious to show his passengers in and around the city.

Our first stop was at a cafe where we sampled delicious pastries and steaming hot, strong coffee. Half-hour later, we walked several blocks away from the city centre and arrived at a courtyard surrounded by brick buildings. The buildings, four-storied high, encircled the entire courtyard, and were adorned with colourful flags. The outside walls of the buildings were painted in vivid colours. As we looked from the windows to the perimeter of the building, one concluded it was used in earlier days as an army barracks.

Carefully treading up several wide steps of heavy stone slabs, we looked down into a black dungeon. Due to the political strive in the mid-1930s between the north and south provinces, we asked our driver if in bygone days it was used to hold prisoners. His face showed a puzzled look, as though he did not wish to answer the question. With a slight nod of his head we sensed, perhaps, this might have been the case. Not wishing to entangle his "cause" or risk answering more questions, he moved us back to the city centre to the next place of interest, the art gallery.

There was little time to spare for window shopping, as our driver urged us to move along. I looked inside a window showing a pair of elegant high-heel shoes I wanted to buy. Then I realized it would be tempting folly to make a rushed purchase.

On our ferry journey back to Portsmouth, William and I relaxed in comfortable chairs in the bar lounge, sipping cool drinks. As we chatted about our trip to Bilbao and its places of interest, I casually remarked how I would like to go back there one day and dig deeper in their ancient history, particularly the period during Franco's regime and where he kept his wine cellars.

Christine in Madrid, Spain.

'The only off-putting thing,' I said, 'is having to circumnavigate the Bay to get there. Would I be up to it?'

'Well, you won't know until you try, will you?' William replied, showing little interest in my concern.

Going round the Bay of Biscay was an experience I did not wish to repeat. The seas swells cause passengers to heave each time the ship's bow dives deeper in the ocean and crashes against her side, as she dips and surfaces to gain stability. The gulf's reputation for its gruesome weather and taking the lives of many seafaring men does not invite anyone in its waters, nor does it encourage one to underestimate its strength.

I wondered where our next journey would take us.

Phil Marshall, Caroline, Christine and Paul Marshall in Madrid, 2009.

In 2009, with my granddaughter Christine, we stayed in Madrid, 300 miles WSW of Barcelona. Madrid compared quite favourably with Bilbao (NNE of Madrid near the Bay of Biscay) which I'd visited before. Notwithstanding its beautiful Gothic churches and other art galleries, I found Bilbao a dour place that lacked vitality. Madrid, on the other hand, was a city alive with energy despite high temperatures, causing one to pause and rest when the sun reached its peak. Life in Northern Spain was at a much slower pace. In Madrid, the excitement of the day began after 8 p.m, when we had wined and dined. Closer to midnight, revellers were out in the squares singing, dancing and watching performing artists. Despite the cooler evenings, the humidity caused onlookers to mop brows.

NEAR MISSES

In the post-war years, this catch-up game between the two of us was in reversed sequence, to a mouse dodging the cat. Whenever William was home in Hampshire, I was abroad. On the other hand, if I happened to be in England my brother was stationed at some far-flung foreign port, serving his country. For years, we had uncontrollable near misses. I reasoned, by the time we reached our ultimate goal, brother and sister would be too old to travel.

Two years after emigrating to Canada in 1967, for the second time, my family and I moved into a new housing development in Mississauga, Ontario. It was a small community of several hundred thousand people and in 1968 it was incorporated as the Town of Mississauga. In 1974 the City of Mississauga was incorporated through the amalgamation of the Town of Mississauga and the villages of Port Credit and Streetsville. It has grown to be Canada's sixth largest city.

Today, that once small town is heavily populated to over one million. Within its borders stand large factories of well-known companies who employ workers living in and out of the city. During the eighteen years I lived in Mississauga the thought of industries and housing developments, stretching from the borders of Bolton, Brampton, and further north of the City, would be unimaginable.

William and Violet often visited the house in Mississauga. I had become the proud owner of my first car, a Plymouth, painted cherry red. With spit and polish, and tender loving care, I treated it like a new born babe. My driving skills began late in life, despite the urge, in earlier years, to learn to drive and take the wheel of a car at all cost. Making several attempts to qualify as a driver, I eventually succeeded after my third one. My driving instructor, skilled in the rudiments of road rules, enthusiastically encouraged me when leaving the parking spot, with 'give gas and go.' I held on to the wheel as I hit the accelerator.

My first driving test, on a bitterly cold winter day, was to follow my instructor's rules, diligently, to the book. This resulted with the examiner and the learner ending up with the nose of the car precariously balanced, at the edge of a ditch on Dundas Street in Mississauga. Satan could not have picked a worse day for a driving test. Slippery roads and heavy snow made driving difficult at best for the experienced driver never mind the learner, as the wind shield wipers continued to clank back and forth before my eyes.

The examiner grudgingly took over the wheel, eased the car on the road, and drove back to the examination centre. With nerves on edge, I entered the office and stood at the counter waiting for the results of my test. Shuffling paperwork on the opposite side of the counter, the examiner looked at me and shook his head.

Out of the blue I stuttered, 'Don't suppose I passed?'

Without a word he fled the scene as though his backside was scorched, perhaps realizing with his lucky escape he still had one of his "cat's nine lives" left to enjoy.

When I related my driving experience and the test taken with a certain examiner whom I never saw again, my brother absolutely loved the story. Often on country roads we stopped at farms to look at the cattle and horses. As we meandered along, his comment never failed to be, 'Hope you realize the precious cargo you are carrying.'

I grinned at him through the rear view mirror, while trying to keep my eyes on the road ahead, not wishing to end up in a ditch, in the middle of nowhere.

Often William arranged his visits to coincide with the Highland Games at Fergus, Ontario, held during the hot, humid summer months. Taking umbrellas and enough food and water to last the day, we left the house early in the morning with the hope of reaching Fergus before the crowds appeared so we could find a sheltered spot close enough to the tall oak and cedar trees, and a parking spot. In the grounds were long wooden benches, erected in layers of four, to accommodate the hundreds of expected visitors. Often, latecomers found all spaces on the benches were taken so had to resort to finding room on the grass and if lucky enough to have brought a chair, were able to sit at a spot closer to the games. Without a shaded area and if not wearing a hat, the sun beat unmercifully on our heads. One year, we arrived for the Games late to find there were no parking spots left, or cool trees to sit under. We parked the car on a side street, outside the gates. Once inside the gates we chose an area where visitors were allowed to sit on the dry grass. Putting rugs and blankets on the grass we settled down to enjoy the Games. Despite wearing large hats for protection from the sun, when we left the grounds noses and chins showed signs of pink as an upcoming sunburn. We reached home happy, tired and hot, and agreed the Games were as good as last year. Then, we set to, with cotton wool and calamine lotion to sooth faces and noses.

Although William was used to climatic conditions in the Mediterranean areas of Gibraltar and Malta and different parts in the Far East when serving in the Navy, he found the humidity of Ontario unbearably hot. Particularly so at the games in Fergus, where he could be seen constantly mopping his brow.

One year at the Games, I purchased a shield of the Marshall/Keith clan from one of the many stalls promoting Scottish kilts and other goods made in the Highlands. The shield started life more than 150 years ago when it was planted in Scotland as an oak seedling. The Chief of Keith, the Rt. Hon. The Earl of Kintore, whose motto *Veritas vincit* (Truth

Prevails), is shown on the back of the shield. When I presented the gift to William, for once he was speechless! The shield is now in safe-keeping in my possession until one day, it will go to Daniel his eldest son.

The summer and fall Fergus markets are crowded to the point it requires an effort to get from one stall to the next, without being crushed. I had one thought in my head: to buy all the fruit and vegetables I could, to preserve for the winter months ahead.

When William finally left the Navy, on both sides of the Atlantic our lives became a little less frantic. Whatever plans were made to meet up with each other, this catch-up game finally ended.

BRUTAL ASSAULT

In 1981, I received dreadful news from my eldest sister Kathleen who was living in Riverside, California. She had been brutally assaulted. I heard the sound of sniffs and gasps as she asked over the phone if I would ring William and come with him to see her. I rang William immediately with the details, and he had no qualms in making flight arrangements from London to the then major airport Malton, Ontario. I said I would pick him up when his plane arrived.

I asked if he would fill me in with particulars of the flight carrier, time, and date of arrival so I could book flights for both of us to Los Angeles with an American airline, two days after his arrival. Our flight took off in the morning, and we were pleasantly surprised to be served a hot meal. Upon arriving at Los Angeles we picked up our luggage and walking through the sliding door on our way out, our sister was waiting to greet us.

We were shocked in disbelief to see her face covered in bruises, her eyes swollen beyond recognition. I was almost on the verge of tears when William took charge by hugging Kathleen, saying, 'we'll sort things out for you, don't worry.'

Guiding us out of the airport to where she had parked her car, we scrambled in the seats as my sister took the wheel and headed to her home in Riverside, at least an hour long journey away. Throughout the drive, none of us spoke of the event that had caused such brutality. When we reached her home, set in a rural area, we settled down with cups of coffee and remained silent until my sister was ready to fill us in with the details of her attack.

Rather than worry about dinner that day, William suggested we all take off somewhere for a leisurely meal. We went to a restaurant where excellent food was served. The walls inside were covered in pictures large and small of Hollywood stars. I was mesmerized by the way each picture blended with the one next to it but what was more astonishing, the eyes of the stars stared in your face at whichever angle you gazed at them. It was an uncanny feeling. I wondered if the artwork was deliberately displayed on the walls to encourage diners back to the restaurant. That being the motive, it was a brilliant piece of marketing and most effective.

After dinner, we stayed up till the late hours of the night talking about plans to protect and safeguard the house from intruders. The following morning we arranged to see the Sheriff who was dealing with the assault case. An officer in splendid uniform arrived at the house and took us by car to the Sheriff's office where he showed us, without going through the preliminaries, photographs taken of my sister's face after the attack. As we listened to the officer who went out of his way to give us the information we asked, we were devastated by this recent event, and I was feeling nauseous. There were no words to describe how a person could, without compunction, be so brutal to another.

We arrived back at our sister's home and spent the afternoon lapping up the sunshine in her garden. We had no wish to intrude by asking questions about the day of the attack, and thought it best to let her tell us in her own good time what she recalled on that dreadful night.

The investigation by the Sheriff's office was not producing the results they hoped for, despite making extensive inquiries in the neighbourhood if any other residents had been attacked or their homes broken into. The Sheriff's one aim was to find the guilty party quickly before another woman was assaulted. Meanwhile, the investigations continued and still no charges had been laid. Making a return visit to the neighbour living next door, the officer had an uncanny feeling the man's signed statement of his whereabouts during the early hours of the morning when the attack took place did not make sense. With each inquiry the neighbour's story changed.

The Sheriff did not let up. He was an officer who felt it his duty to solve this heinous crime and bring the assailant to justice. A few more days went by, and after grilling the neighbour next door to substantiate his statement over and over, he was finally able to make him break down and confess. He was a 40-year-old ex-Marine who had served his country with distinction.

To earn extra money he did odd jobs for my sister, and knew the layout of her house. On the night in question of the attack, he entered through the cat flap entry on the back door and eased his hand up to the latch to let himself in. For no reason at all, he went to my sister's bedroom and began his assault. As she faced his on-going lashes to her face and body, hearing a noise, the intruder fled the scene and left behind a woman's red high heel shoe. It was her cat returning from a night of mice raiding who prevented further brutal assault and came back inside the house at a crucial time which not only saved my sister's life, but prevented the attacker from raping her, no doubt.

When the Marine was finally charged, and faced the judge in court, he was given a thirteen years sentence, with no parole. After the case was heard in court, the Sheriff and his officers continued to visit my sister. It transpired when the investigation probed deeper into the reason of the attack the assailant admitted, under interrogation, the reason he committed the crime was due to a discord with his girlfriend and he chose the nearest person to him to vent his anger of passion. His girlfriend, when questioned by the Sheriff about the character of the Marine, revealed he liked dressing in women's clothing and was particularly fond of wearing high heel shoes. She said the red shoes belonged to her.

Weeks after the court case, several police officers from the station called in to check on my sister. William and I went to the local hardware stores and bought new safety locks for all the doors, including one for her bedroom. All the windows were installed with metal bars that allowed them to open a certain way, but were locked so no one could force entry. The cat flap on the back door was held on a spring which, when opened a certain way, allowed the cat to come in, then clamped back in place to avoid re-entry.

William double-checked all doors and windows to make sure the safety locks and window bars worked. Before returning to Canada, we filled her kitchen cupboards with a variety of foods and vegetables so there was no need for her to shop, for a few weeks. On our journey back to Los Angeles to catch our plane to Toronto, we left with a heavy heart and hoped there would be no repeat of the devastating assault on Kathleen. In the ensuing months medical treatment for her injuries were mounting at an alarming rate, which caused her further stress. I rang her daily after William returned to his family in England. Throughout one conversation we had, she said her medical bills were running so high she was unable to pay them. She had no life insurance and despite being the victim of a heinous crime, it did not warrant help from a governing body. She was expected to pay all her medical expenses. In a conversation with my brother, we agreed to pick up the bills and forward a draft to her in US dollars. It was an episode in our lives we hoped never to be repeated.

An officer who had taken a shine to my sister, without making any previous plans to ask, appeared at her door a short time after William and I returned to Canada, with a Doberman puppy. Kathleen was dumbstruck as she looked from the officer to the dog and without further ado took the animal from his arms, and thanked him for his caring generosity.

Some months later I revisited California and again was met at Los Angeles airport by my sister. The bruising and swelling on her face was fading slightly, but there was a look of nervousness as she checked each passenger coming through arrivals. We gave each other a hug and, reaching her home, the Doberman was eager to sniff the visitor coming through the fenced gate.

'Won't hurt you,' said Kathleen, 'but no one can get near the property with him around.'

I was tempted to say,' Good dog,' but left it at that!

It was not long after this visit my sister decided to sell the property, taking the Doberman with her, and moved to a location further away from Riverside. She went to Sunset City. It was an extraordinary co-incident she located to this area. Although she swore never again to trust men, ironically, she met up with the doctor who attended to her injuries and distraught state of mind after the attack, who had uprooted to the same location and set up a medical clinic.

The doctor she dated, but that is another story.

Kathleen was a beautiful, stylish lady who deserved the best!

TURN OF EVENTS

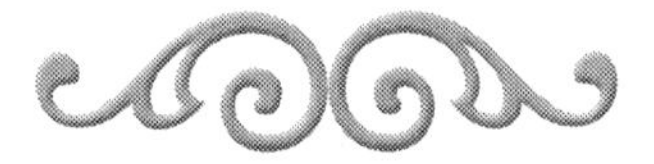

In early September 2006, once again I was flying Air Canada on an overnight flight to Heathrow, London. I was not to realize this would be my last visit to Hampshire. The aircraft touched down on the tarmac in brilliant sunshine, the sky clear blue, and the air pleasantly warm. Weary passengers left the aircraft, while I stayed on board until an assistant came with a wheelchair, and trundled it on the elevator to enter the terminal on the upper level and line up to clear through customs and immigration. Being in a wheelchair, I didn't stand in line while custom officials checked passports and asked the usual questions how long a traveller is likely to stay in the country. To one side of the checkout room, wheelchairs are given priority, which lessens the stress of the passenger when trying to get feet back on solid ground.

My luggage, tagged with a priority label on it, allowed the airport assistant to find it quickly as it came off the revolving belt. This service through Air Canada is excellent. Unfortunately, due to regulations, a grateful traveller is not allowed to give a gratuity for this service.

As we entered through the arrival doors, and seeing my usual taxi driver waiting to greet me with a wide smile on his face, I thanked the assistant for helping me, as she took charge of the wheelchair, and left. The driver picked up my suitcase, and asked if I had a good flight. We walked a short way to where he parked his car in the drafty terminal. Opening the front side door of the car to help me in, I slid in the seat beside him. Leaving the terminal we crawled through heavy traffic before turning off, towards Hampshire. I was glad to be away from the thronging crowds at the airport which I no longer recognized as London, as I listened to foreign tongues and people young and old wearing clothes that would have been considered most unsuitable for travellers, years ago.

Of my many trips to England over the years, this one proved the most tiring. I found myself becoming vexed when having to go through the rituals of security and immigration when leaving my country, then go through the whole procedure again, when arriving at another. In anticipation of leaving the airport, I could hardly wait to see the patchwork of fields and grazing animals, as we headed to the countryside.

Conversation between the driver and passenger was at a lull. It seemed the driver was anxious to keep a conversation going but my thoughts were with William, whom I sensed when last speaking with him over the telephone, was not his usual flamboyant self. I chided myself why I was feeling so low, on a bright sunny day.

We arrived in record time at Waterlooville and being the norm when taking an overnight flight, I wanted to put my head down. Once inside William's apartment I knew it was not possible. He would want to talk, as past visits reminded me, and once we were seated in armchairs in the living room, the chatter would flow non-stop, late in the night.

I reflect back to those times and appreciate the value of how we connected as family. I am glad patience prevailed when I wanted to nap, at the drop of a pin. These memories are now what is left to remind me how close brother and sister were.

Prior to this visit William did not mention he had booked the Crown for two weeks during my month's stay with him. I did not ask. But a few days after arriving, out of the blue he said, 'Well, we had better start packing.'

Our driver, punctual as ever, rang the bell to say he had arrived and when the door was opened, he came in and picked up our luggage. Half-way to Dorset, we stopped at a country pub for lunch close to the New Forest, where ponies lingered to gaze on passing vehicles and travellers whose interest was to explore the National Trust forest. William drank a lager, no whisky, and appeared preoccupied.

Concerned, I asked, 'Are you all right?'

A nod of the head was his response. But somehow I was not completely convinced it was so. We arrived at the Crown in Weymouth and after extending thanks to our driver, said we would see him in two weeks. The first few days went remarkably well as we relaxed on the beach and dined in the hotel restaurant, seeing well-known faces of staff and visitors over the years. As usual, when coming to Weymouth, William made arrangements with a friend to play snooker in the pools hall on Wednesday afternoon for an hour or two. This gave me the opportunity to look round the shops, then meet up with him at the appointed place and time. Snooker gave him time to relax, as he watched the different colour balls roll over the green baize table and with luck, fall into one of the holes either end.

It was in the early hours in the morning of our second week, he awoke with chest pains. Calling out to me for help I hurriedly put on a housecoat and phoned the night porter for an ambulance. By the time the ambulance arrived I had dressed and was putting a heavy robe and a blanket over William. The journey to the hospital seemed a never-ending drive and in desperation I called to one of the ambulance men and asked him where we were going.

'Dorchester,' was his reply.

When the ambulance reached the hospital, William was taken into emergency. What caused me to fluster was the length of time it took a doctor to come to examine him. When he did eventually arrive, he remarked William would need to stay in the hospital for a few days. I returned to the hotel by bus, had a light breakfast, then decided to take a stroll along the beach thinking it would give me the stamina to cope with the days ahead, without him.

Each morning I caught the bus from the town centre of Weymouth that stopped outside Dorchester Hospital and stayed with William till 3 p.m., when I travelled back the same way to Weymouth. The countryside of Dorset is breath-taking, if only a blade of grass that stirs in the wind, or the joy of watching young lambs skirting the hedges in leaps and bounds, exuding energy.

Hampshire is a county in Southern England. Due to its long association with pigs and boars, natives of the county have been known as Hampshire Hogs since the 18th century. Arts connections include being the birthplace of Charles Dickens, Jane Austen and Charles Kingsley and noted landscaper painter J.M.W. Turner. The New Forest is known for its ponies which roam freely. It has a mosaic of heathland, grassland, deciduous woodland habitat that host diverse wildlife, including domesticated cattle, pigs, horse and several wild deer species. Hampshire lies outside the green belt area of restricted development around London, but has good railway and motorway links to the capital.

For the rest of my stay at Weymouth, I travelled daily to the hospital, and as my visit was drawing ever closer I worried about retrieving the remains of my personal belongings, including my Canadian passport left in William's apartment, before flying back. I approached his doctor at the hospital with the need to get my brother safely in his home at the earliest, and to enable me leave Dorset to pick up my possessions. He was sympathetic and said if I promised on the way back to Waterlooville, to make several stops to give him a rest, and for him to see his own doctor at the first opportunity, he would agree.

In making arrangements to return to Waterlooville I phoned our taxi driver who was sympathetic with the news and appreciated the reason for our change of plans. I told him a friend with whom William played Wednesday snooker at the pools hall, and his wife, who visited daily, would pick William up at the hospital and return to the hotel for me. My appreciative thanks go out to this caring couple who ensured we arrived back safely in Waterlooville.

After our goodbyes, and William was settled in his own bed, I phoned his doctor with the news of his condition. He arrived the next morning and after examining my brother, told me he had to go back in hospital, and he would ring for the ambulance right away. My brother's face was contorted with pain and when I ask where it hurt, he pointed to the right side of his body. He had pneumonia. An ambulance arrived and took him to St. Mary's in Portsmouth. This daily journey took me much longer to reach the hospital and left me with palpitations that convinced me I would never recover, as each day nearer to leaving England, caused further stress.

St. Mary's was a depressing hospital, old, and its corridors painted dark green were enough to unbalance the healthiest of people. It is my understanding it was demolished a few years ago but of plans to build on this piece of land, I have no knowledge.

William was released two days prior to my journey back home. He looked pale and fragile, as though every spark of energy had been drained from his body. On the day of my departure, I hugged him as though not wanting to let go. Our taxi driver arrived, and came in to pick up my luggage, I gave a final farewell and said to William, 'Without fail, I will be back next March and stay as long as you wish so I can take care of you.'

On my journey home to Canada, I was full of foreboding with thoughts of the agony William was now facing. This prompted me to ring a neighbourly friend living in the same building as him. I asked her if she would keep an eye on him and perhaps pop in occasionally to see if he was all right.

Christmas was fast approaching and when I rang to find out how he was, I sensed the celebration of the season was far from his mind. His youngest son Ralph had called in, bringing gifts. Most of his day however was spent in bed. He did not have the strength to get dressed.

On-going telephone calls from this side of the Atlantic were not encouraging as each day seemed to drag into the next, and no further improvement was forthcoming regarding his health. The doctor made frequent house calls and with each one, was of the opinion William should be staying in the hospital. However, William's wish was, 'When the end comes, I want to be in my own home.'

Early March 2007, a neighbour knocked on his front door, which was left unlocked until nightfall, with a tea tray in her hand. She called out his name and when she did not get a reply, put the tray down and went to investigate. William was on his knees in the bathroom, struggling for breath. Immediately, she rang his son who came quickly and phoned for an ambulance. When William arrived at the Queen Alexandra Hospital he was immediately put in extensive care, where he died a few minutes later.

Shock waves went through the building as the neighbours watched the ambulance come and go. Accompanying his father, the younger son stayed with him and when he passed away, phoned his sister and elder brother. No one had the courtesy, or care, to ring Darlene in Nottingham, who was still his wife, until after the Will was read by William's solicitor.

The same neighbour with whom I became friendly on my visits to William, told me the following day the family came in and were seen taking boxes by the load out of the apartment. Her comment: 'like vultures picking meat off thin bones.'

I was advised by the solicitors my brother had left me his complete set of volumes of first issues stamps going back to 1946, along with old English coins. My niece, the daughter of my eldest brother Rowland, offered to bring them with her when she visited her father in British Columbia, months later. I knew Darlene had been left her husband's large old clock and two Victorian vases she admired. These were sent to her after probate of the Will.

Daniel, with his wife and small child, arrived in Portsmouth from America, to attend the funeral. Because of the irreconcilable difference between Darlene and his brother and sister, he chose not to sit with them at the service, but with Darlene. He was of the opinion from the day his father met and married her, she had been given a raw deal by the rest of the family. I did not attend the funeral. It would have been too painful for me to see his coffin placed in front of the altar, and covered with the Union Jack flag; his bravery and service medals sitting on top.

William's death left an indescribable void in my life, one I never thought possible. I was no longer interested in taking yearly flights across the Atlantic, and sat for many hours going over memories of the numerous trips we took together. There would be no Sunday long chats over the telephone, laughter, and competing with talents to see which of us could beat the other. No longer would there be visits to Asda in Waterlooville where he chivvied up the ladies to meet him under the old railway clock. The wily red-tail fox who crossed our path, as we strolled arm in arm toward the golf club for dinner. Trips to Weymouth where we travelled across unspoiled landscape of the Dorset countryside, often stopping to watch the Clydesdales pull cartloads of hay.

Of the many gifts bestowed on me over the years, I treasure a carriage clock, precious pearls, a set of antique silver spoons and a gold wrist-watch. These I hold dear, not for what they are worth in monetary gain, but because they came from William, a man with a generous heart. Not only had I lost a caring brother, but also my best friend.

MAN UNTO HIMSELF

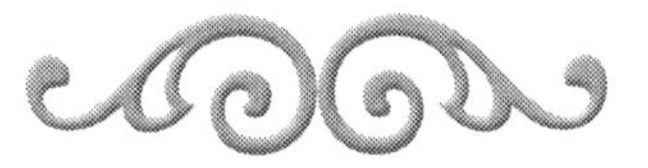

In the final analysis, looking back over the years on the rare occasion when William was philosophical in thought, I realized his intelligence in summing up situations that were about to happen, was extraordinary. Although it was like pulling teeth to get him to talk about his life in the Navy, he did "open up" if he thought *The Official Secrets Act* was not being threatened, and there was no possibility of finding himself jailed through careless talk. At one time, years after the war, when returning home to Waterlooville from a trip to Isle of Wight via Portsmouth, he conveyed to me there was an underground tunnel stemming from The Solent near Portsmouth, where communications were set-up to determine ships coming and going, covering all regions of The English Channel. Even listening to this type of skulduggery that went on throughout the Second World War, I held my tongue, fearful, not to let slip even this minute piece of information.

On my many visits to him, we often sat late in the night chatting about our families. Not only did he bestow great affection on his family, but also on mine. During our conversations he conveyed his admiration to his brother and sisters on their remarkable life achievements in a society where class distinction in the UK in the 1920s and later reared its head to those less endowed, who, through no fault of their own, found themselves groping in dark corners, to survive.

Many times he told me, 'You would have been a good politician, because you are a people's person and forever fighting for the underdog.'

To which I answered, 'There but for the Grace of God, go I.'

I knew there was much more to add to this comment, but it would serve no useful purpose. In my younger years, I had ambitions to be a politician, and become involved at all levels of government in Canada.

I held my tongue and reflected on this philosophical thought: 'When opportunity knocks and one is denied, to reflect on what might or might not have been, determines the path of one's life.'

When it came to being serious with the ladies, William appeared to border on the edge of paranoia. Consider his two love affairs – and I feel sure there were many other light-hearted ladies whom he dated after his marriage of 44 years to Violet – something caused him to have a change of heart when hearing the sound of wedding bells in his ears. Although he did marry Darlene, in face of his family's objections, I sensed William regretted he did not hold on to his second wife, as he spoke of her in endearing words and told me they rang each other weekly.

Marion, who passed away in his arms in the Isle of Wight, I believe he would eventually have married. In retrospect, however, with her being a lady of class and some years older, he may have thought she would try to change his character. To put in his own words, 'It was not on!'

In his life he was happy to "play" with the ladies and keep them dangling on strings, knowing full well all invites to meet him under the old railway clock were never to materialize. Listening to many of the Asda ladies I was fully aware they too were playing the same game and egging him on, with their spouses standing close by and hard pressed restraining themselves from retorting fully to William's rhetoric advances.

He was a man unto himself. I loved him dearly. He is sorely missed.

ABOUT THE AUTHOR

CAROLINE WHITEHEAD was born in London, England, and raised in an orphanage in Kent. Knowing the importance of family relationships, she pushed forward for forty years to discover her brothers' and sisters' identities, overcoming many obstacles so the siblings could experience those ties – and their stories could finally be told in a sequence of three books.

Married in 1944, she emigrated to Canada in 1967 and lived in Ontario before moving to British Columbia in 1987. Her husband died in 1999. She has one daughter, three grandchildren, two great-grandchildren, and a wealth of proud memories.

Manufactured by Amazon.ca
Bolton, ON